Praise for
Make Waves and Patti Johnson

"*Make Waves* empowers readers to become everyday leaders by enacting real change in their lives, communities, and businesses. Johnson encourages asking "how can I help" and "what can I do" to bring tangible transformation to fruition. You'll find this book provides meaningful tools for any aspiring 'wave maker' to take charge and embody the change they want to see in the world."

—Doug Conant, chairman, Avon Products; chairman, Kellogg Executive Leadership Institute; founder & CEO, Conant Leadership; former president & CEO, Campbell Soup Company; co-author of the NYT best seller *Touchpoints: Creating Powerful Leadership Connections in the Smallest of Moments*

"*Make Waves* provides a unique and incredibly motivating approach to taking on a change. Change, no matter large or small, personal or professional, can seem daunting and Patti's book causes you to think that you can make a difference in a meaningful way. Patti's guidance causes you to step back, think, and get inspired to act. The book is just the right amount of how-to and inspiration. A must-read."

—Maria Cramer, vice president, Hitachi Consulting

"*Make Waves* is a wonderful narrative on change and how to most effectively navigate through it, with both real-world and practical examples. In a world of increasing change and growing complexity, it serves as a great resource to help manage through both the personal and professional changes everyone experiences. It avoids the all-too-common pitfalls of delving into the overly theoretical or academic; rather, it is a great balance of real-world examples that one can apply in all settings."

—David Nashif, vice president, Change Leadership, McKesson

"In *Make Waves*, Patti Johnson answers the question, "What is leadership?" Her writing is filled with the stories of real leaders and real leadership. This is a must-read book for anyone who has a wave that he or she needs to make!"

—Larry Peters, professor of Management & Leadership Development, Neeley School of Business, Texas Christian University

"Who better from whom to learn the art of change than Patti Johnson, a veteran of management consulting giant Accenture and a self-made wave maker? *Make Waves* proves that lighting that match is not just for high-profile people. Each of us has the power and ability to transform our lives, jobs, and organizations in incredible ways."

—Alexandra Levit, business & workplace consultant
and author of *Blind Spots: The 10 Business Myths You Can't Afford to Believe*

"*Make Waves* is a fun and informative book that challenges each of us to find places in our lives where we can be positively disruptive. There are a lot of business books that provide great theories and models for personal change and transformation but Patti Johnson is able to transition from conceptual to practical and demonstrates how everyday individuals found the power to bring positive changes to their work, schools, and communities. This book serves as a reminder that everyone can move from being a spectator to an active participant in bring about positive changes. A great read for corporate leaders, early career individuals, and students."

—Miya Maysent, vice president,
7-Eleven, Inc.

"Want to make change, but completely unsure how to pull it off—or even, maybe, where to start? Drop everything and read Patti Johnson's phenomenal, inspirational new book, *Make Waves*. Her formula—Think, Know, Do—is simple without being simplistic. Rather, it's the essential how-to manual for those among us who thirst to bring needed change to our teams, our organizations, our communities, or maybe even our world. Savor every page. Scribble your notes. Read, Plan, Act. Make your own waves!"

—Ted Coine, author, keynote speaker,
and co-founder Switch and Shift

"I always challenge my clients and audiences by asking: What are you doing today to help future business leaders who have yet to be born? In *Make Waves*, Patti Johnson shares pragmatic principles and practical tools to get us started on the journey of leaving a positive lasting legacy wherever we are in the workplace and marketplace."

—K. Shelette Stewart, PhD,
associate director,
SMU Cox Executive Education

"The personal and pragmatic approach to the topic of change was really refreshing. Leveraging wave makers, their stories, their insights, and their words brought to life the impact that we can each make when we embrace the opportunity to make a difference. I found myself being deliberate about embracing my own professional opportunity to be a wave maker. The assignment that was initially a task now has the potential to be a wave with much broader impact. So I'm off to embrace my wave opportunity, challenge conventional wisdom, and engage idea partners to collaborate on creating change."

—Susan Barnicoat, senior director,
PepsiCo

MAKE WAVES

MAKE WAVES

Be the One to Start Change
at Work and in Life

Patti Johnson

First published by Bibliomotion, Inc.
39 Harvard Street
Brookline, MA 02445
Tel: 617-934-2427
www.bibliomotion.com

Printed in the United States of America

10 9 8 7 6 5 4 3 2

Library of Congress Cataloging-in-Publication Data

Johnson, Patti.
    Make waves : be the one to start change at work and in life / by Patti Johnson.
        pages cm
    Includes bibliographical references and index.
    ISBN 978-1-937134-91-4 (hardcover : alk. paper) — ISBN 978-1-937134-92-1 (ebook) —
ISBN 978-1-937134-93-8 (enhanced ebook)
    1. Organizational change.   2. Change (Psychology)   3. Altruism.   4. Social action.
I. Title.
    HD58.8.J645 2014
    650.1—dc23
                                          2014001064

To my family, who has encouraged and supported me over the past two years in making this book a reality. You help me keep perspective and remember what really matters in life. And, you never let me forget that laughter makes everything better.

Contents

Acknowledgments

Love and gratitude to my husband, Jim, who I could never have written this book without. He has been encouraging and supportive of me every single day.

Thank you to Erika Heilman and Jill Friedlander for their commitment to "the wave" and seeing the possibilities. And, a special thank you to their team and partners, Ari Choquette, Shevaun Betzler, and Jill Schoenhaut, as well as Rusty Shelton and his group. Gratitude to Susan Lauzau who, along with Erika, offered such wise and careful guidance on the manuscript and coached me through my first book. I have felt part of a vital author community and that has helped me beyond measure.

Special thank you to my amazing PeopleResults friends and partners for being there with so much support, interest, and wisdom. An extra thank you to Kristi Erickson for being a constant sounding board, insightful reviewer, and an enthusiastic supporter.

I appreciate Josh Getzler for believing in the book before it was fully formed and helping me make it a reality. And, thank you to Lauren Murphy for encouraging my very first step.

A heartfelt thank you to so many dear friends who have encouraged me, listened to me, and shown such support through my writing adventure.

A big thanks to my brother, Mike, for being my "short posse" and rolling up his sleeves to help. And, thank you to my son, Patrick, for being my motivator and using my own advice back on me at just the right time! Love and thanks to my son Will, who read, reviewed, and cared.

Finally, thank you to my Mom and Dad for more than I can count, as well as Allison and Matt. Also, gratitude to Helen Johnson, my mother-in-law, for helping me see the wave through different eyes.

My life has been blessed with so many friends, family, and colleagues who took the time to offer wise counsel, make an introduction, and care when I needed it most. I am grateful to each of you.

Make Waves

Be the One to Start Change at Work and in Life

THINK

Find your wave

Think like a wave maker

KNOW

Challenge conventional wisdom

Incorporate trends

DO

Create lasting change

Create a community

PART 1

What You Think

Find your wave

- Ask "what if...?"
- Know your gifts
- Know what makes a wave

Think like a wave maker

- See the unseen
- View opportunity vs. risk
- Ask, "what can I do?"
- Know what you don't know
- Think progress, not perfection
- Tackle fears and assumptions
- Understand Wave Maker DNA

THINK

CHAPTER 1

What's Your Wave?

Don't make waves. Blend in. Wait your turn. Unless you want to start a change that matters—one that makes a real difference. Your career and contribution to the world depend on it.

Think of a "wave" as any change that begins with your decision to act and ripples outward, or as the transfer of energy that creates momentum and ultimately a positive impact. It may be a small decision or action at first, building as it goes.

Some waves are far reaching. Some are small ripples at first. Some waves happen inside organizations, while others sweep over a larger community or marketplace. The common denominator is that one person saw a need or opportunity and decided to be the one to start a change.

And, waves don't have to begin with those who have the most important title or the greatest experience. The new professional, the first-time entrepreneur, the student, or the leader in a Fortune 500 company can all start a meaningful change.

FINDING YOUR WAVE

What change is waiting for you? When you come home, how do you finish the sentence, "If only we could..."? Finding your wave is essential to creating meaning in your work, building an impactful career, and turning your dreams into reality.

All around you, you see opportunities for impactful change. They're at work and in your community—you see a neighborhood in need, a better way for your team to work, a new business idea, or a group of people who can help one another reach their goals.

The opportunity lies in the connection between what the world needs and what you can do. You have to see opportunity before you can make your wave happen. And it will take action from you.

> "Companies don't disrupt, people do."
> —*Whitney Johnson*, Dare, Dream, Do[1]

Sure, there are some huge waves that we've all experienced. Steve Jobs was a Wave Maker™ who had an astounding impact on our culture and technology. His change was bigger than almost anyone could have imagined. But the size and impact of Steve Jobs's wave is no reason to miss yours.

Waves are as unique as you are. You have something special to contribute. This book is written for you, whether your wave is big or small. We all have waves within us.

A VERY PERSONAL WAVE MAKER

Before we dive in, let me share my perspective on making waves, which changed after a very personal experience. Call it an "aha moment" or a turning point, after which I saw this book, and change, through a different lens. You see, for many years, my family had an up-close look at someone who made waves. And even though she is gone, her ripple effects continue. She was a true Wave Maker.

Last year, I received an urgent call from my husband, Jim. His mother, the matriarch of the family, had just had a massive heart attack. I knew from the tone of Jim's voice that time was running out. Helen Johnson was a force of nature; full of ideas and plans, she was the center of the family. On that hot summer evening we looked at each other sadly, wondering what we'd do without her.

More family arrived and we sat around Helen's huge oak dining table, as we had so many Sunday lunches and holidays in the past. We began to do what all families do at such times: we shared stories about her life and heard many new ones from friends and neighbors who came by to remember her too.

As a young girl, Helen had worked two and three jobs to put herself through college, and her siblings pooled their savings to ensure they all reached this goal too. She found her life's work as a sixth-grade teacher, and she helped hundreds of children who needed not only guidance in the classroom but an adult who cared about them and shared supplies, encouragement, and support.

She and her husband, Ed, were heartbroken when he was diagnosed with Alzheimer's disease upon his retirement. But Helen soon became an Alzheimer's support group leader and she bolstered countless others when their loved ones received this devastating diagnosis. In her darkest hour, she made the decision to help others.

Despite her disappointments, Helen never lost her zest and love of life. She started a seniors group in her church, continued to take college classes and share what she learned with others, and tried social media because she wanted to be where her kids and grandkids were. She was always excitedly planning the next destination for her travel group, was the first to organize a get-together in honor of a friend, and was there for family members when they needed her most.

As we shared stories about Helen's decisions and actions, which didn't seem that significant when she made them, we realized that her ripple effects were astounding. Her decisions to help in so many situations started changes and reactions that went well beyond what she even knew.

Her ripples started with some very simple questions. In every situation, she asked herself, "What can I do?" and "How can I help?" Then, the hard part—she did it. Her habit of accountability and her bias for action are powerful lessons in how just one person can start important changes. Her actions led to significant changes not just in the groups she was part of, but in the lives of others, encouraging and lifting them up when they needed it most.

After the services, I dedicated myself to researching and studying individuals who have made waves. I asked trusted colleagues, "Who do you know that is a Wave Maker?" Many animatedly told me about people who had inspired them by starting big or small changes. I eagerly anticipated the interviews because of my colleagues' enthusiasm in nominating their Wave Makers. They did not disappoint. I was riveted by stories of how these individuals began and sustained their changes, both big and small. After many conversations, I identified twenty-four Wave Makers to feature in this book. I studied their outlook, as well as the decisions they made and the actions they took when starting their changes. I hope their experiences will be as instructional and inspiring to you as they were to me.

WAVES BEGIN WITH "IF ONLY WE COULD..."

Let me share a few examples of how one person's actions started a wave, either big or small. They all began with "If only we could..."

- The college student who organized a way to share wasted campus food with the homeless
- The female manager who built commitment and received funding to start a networking group that connects younger female professionals to senior mentors
- The young engineer with an idea for a process change that no one had considered, yet it improved both productivity and customer service
- The company vice president who translated her growth strategy into simple and clear outcomes, engaging more than three thousand employees to make the vision a reality
- The math teacher who convinced the school district to introduce an advanced math curriculum to better prepare students for college

These are diverse examples, and the planning and execution of each wave was different because of its varying scale and complexity. Yet, there are many common themes in the way the individuals who started these changes think, act, and engage with others.

Throughout this book, we'll meet an eclectic group of Wave Makers who led a variety of changes that made life better for those around them. Clint Hurdle's wave was changing the culture in a Major League clubhouse; Emma Scheffler, while a high school freshman, started a charity to help children and their families fearful about a diabetes diagnosis; and Brett Hurt's wave was creating a new company based on open sharing of customer opinions and views.

We'll learn from each of them as well as many others.

LEARNING ABOUT WAVES

Make Waves is based on the belief that we can all learn from one another's waves. I believe that a university professor's innovative way of creating a learning community is relevant for the new graduate; that a student's founding of a community event that has grown for more than twenty-five years has relevance outside a college setting; and that an entrepreneur's successful start-up holds valuable insights for leaders in the Fortune 500. Even though each change is different, there are common patterns, habits, and strategies that fuel those who start grassroots changes. Together, we'll explore their meaning and discover how you can use these strategies to start your own wave.

In many ways, starting a wave is more possible today than ever before. While there have been Wave Makers throughout history, there is a major shift underway that is changing how waves start and build momentum. Trends in culture, media, and technology are transforming the way we collaborate and share, which affects how we work together on any change. Access to information is being equalized so that anyone can have the same knowledge and influence, which is leveling hierarchies.

Recent graduates have very different preferences and expectations than those of other generations for how they consume information and engage with one another. They have grown up in a digital social world, able to share instantly with their circle and beyond. Technology options that didn't exist just a few years ago are creating new expectations about how people communicate and work together. It's time to reconsider your old assumptions—we'll examine them here.

After we take a fresh look at possibilities, we'll explore how you actually start your change and build momentum. There isn't a step-by-step formula for starting a wave, but there are strategies to help you and lessons to learn from those who've done it. I always encourage my clients to take touted "best practices" and learn from them, but translate them only if they fit. The same is true for your wave.

Think, too, about the Wave Makers you already know. Who have you watched start a wave? What actions did they take to make it successful? How did they react when their wave hit a wall? Adding your own observations and experiences to the stories in *Make Waves* will bring you new insights, and you'll see that successful waves are happening all around you.

Make Waves is designed to give you the confidence and tools you need to get started and to challenge some of your long-held assumptions. In my work advising leaders about organizational change, I see much conventional wisdom that needs to be revisited; we'll question our beliefs on the traditional way of doing things.

We'll also look at how Wave Makers realized their goals in spite of setbacks and bumps along the way. We'll learn how to assess your setbacks, regroup, and find your Plan B.

WAVES WITHIN WAVES

If you are part of an organization, there is a good chance there are bigger waves happening around you. Businesses are moving into new markets. New technology is changing the way you work. Organizations are growing rapidly, and you are right in the middle of it. Even if someone else started a much bigger change, decide how you can contribute. You can start a change within a bigger wave and be part of making your organization or community better. This mind-set of accountability is an essential part of what Stephen Covey called the Circle of Influence—knowing what you can affect or influence.

WAVE CONDITIONS

As you consider your ideas, think about the ingredients that make a successful wave. Waves have three key criteria:

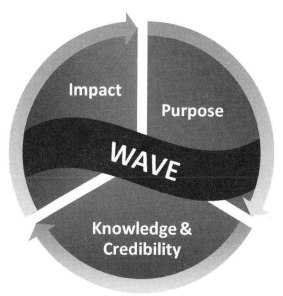

Figure 1–1: Wave Conditions

1. **A wave creates undeniable *impact* at the right time.** A wave's goal is to make your organization, community, or market better with tangible results. The mechanism for change may be offering a new service, helping those in need, improving the customer experience, or creating a new business. A wave has to matter and have the potential to create positive change. And, the "right time" means that an idea is shared when conditions make it possible to succeed—even with resistance. Timing impacts how much attention your change receives, the pace of progress, and readiness for your ideas.

> **"It made it easy for others to buy in once they saw results."**
> —*Jonathan Morris*

2. **A wave has a bigger *purpose* that engages others.** A wave, by design, has ripple effects. It can move forward by way of other people without you guiding every step. This is possible because it has meaning and purpose. We'll learn more in coming chapters about the power of word of mouth and personal recommendations. This advocacy of an idea only happens if it has greater purpose and value that makes a difference.

> **"We tied everything we did to the bigger business strategy."**
> —*Fiona Grant*

3. **A wave is built upon *knowledge* and *credibility*.** Waves require both passion and substance. You have to know your topic. You can become a quick study or invite the right experts to be your partners. You'll need knowledge and expertise as well as credibility to be the champion. Credibility is essential in encouraging others to believe in the cause.

Waves are meaningful, impactful, and start from a core source of knowledge that gives them credibility. But waves start because one person decided. It starts with you.

What if? What if we changed how we grow the business? What if my business could reach customers globally? What if high school students had the knowledge and resources to earn more scholarships? What if my team felt appreciated and valued?

What if? You could be the one to answer this question.

I hope that *Make Waves* will inspire you to:

- Decide your wave
- Understand the power of your thoughts in getting started and staying motivated

- Decide the actions that will start, build momentum for, and sustain your change
- Incorporate new practices, habits, and strategies for starting a change

I wrote this book to encourage you to reflect, learn, and ultimately decide to start making your own waves! You'll notice questions for you to consider as you think about your change. Whenever possible, I avoid using the word "steps," because changes aren't sequential. Waves are more likely to flow, growing and evolving as they move forward. Please read *Make Waves* with the mind-set that you will work on several actions simultaneously. And, of course, you'll have to tailor your approach to your unique situation. Think of this book as a framework or blueprint that will give you the confidence and knowledge you need to get started and realize your goals.

Make Waves is intended to offer you the guidance, stories, examples, and trends that will encourage you to start a meaningful wave in your group, organization, or life—and to gain the confidence to believe that you can do it. We know that change can start from anywhere and with anyone. It just takes one person to take that first step.

It can be you. What's your wave?

THINK TIME

As you read, think about your wave. Here are some questions to consider:

- What would you like to be different in your work or career?
- What would make your organization (club, group, team, committee, network) better?
- What community needs will benefit from your talents and attention?
- What are your passions and interests? How can you use them for a bigger purpose?
- If you could make one difference in the world around you, what would it be?

I encourage you to consider these questions first, so that as you dive into *Make Waves*, you have your wave(s) in mind.

CHAPTER 2

Think Like a Wave Maker

Before we look at how to start your wave, let's consider how you *think* about it. When I began writing this book, this chapter wasn't even in my outline. But after I studied how individuals start successful changes, I concluded that it wasn't just about their actions but about the way they think. I added this chapter when I heard story after story from those who began successful changes and noted their optimism, bias to action, persistence, and adaptability in reaching their goals. Yes, they made smart decisions in how they began and built momentum, but their thoughts powered them from the very beginning.

As part of my research for *Make Waves*, I interviewed many Wave Makers about how they started their changes, including twenty-four featured in this book. Despite the diversity in the scale and impact of their waves, there were underlying common themes in their thinking that gave these Wave Makers the confidence to act.

Major League Baseball Manager Clint Hurdle, of the Pittsburgh Pirates, said, "I believe that everything starts with your thoughts. Your choices are to (a) not think at all; (b) think negatively; or (c) think positively. I choose thinking positively. We all have that choice."

Wave Makers see the unseen opportunity when they start their change. They aren't limited by today or stuck in the status quo. They are open to "what if?" and are committed to reaching their goals. These practical dreamers believe in what they can see, even when others can't.

> "Follow your own internal thermostat more than the external thermostat."
> —*Clint Hurdle*

Those who start changes are much more motivated by the potential impact of their wave than by a desire for recognition. The Wave Makers I spoke with had a passion for their cause—which ranged from promoting good health to improving patient care. While they certainly saw risks and had fears, they didn't let their concerns prevent them from taking action. They were motivated by the belief that the change would make their organization, group, or market better. They also had a commitment to get moving and explore how to make progress. They were passionate, informed, and persistent.

Allen Stephenson, Wave Maker and creator of Southern Tide, an American apparel company, shared his motivation from the beginning of his career, when he was just twenty-two years old. Asked if he had any fears when he started, Allen answered:

> I really didn't. But, I also knew that I had to put everything in to it. That meant I had to give up my social life, give up all my hobbies. I quit school. I had no money, because I spent it all on the business. I moved back into my parents' house. I didn't buy anything and I worked about fifteen to sixteen hours a day, every day, for a couple of years. I knew I could do it; it was just a matter of if I would be dedicated enough. I knew that I would, because, heck, I dropped out of college. So if I screwed up, I wouldn't have had anything to fall back on. And almost no one thought it would work, except for my mom. Almost everyone else thought I was crazy. I don't really care if people think I'm crazy. But the deck was stacked against me in every possible way if I didn't succeed—financially, educationally, socially. I had to do it.

> **"You don't get what you don't ask for."**
> —*Fiona Grant*

I found that those who start and sustain successful changes have a special way of thinking. Wave Makers typically:

- See the unseen
- See the opportunity more than the risks
- Ask, "What can I do?" and take action
- Know what they don't know
- Think progress not perfection
- Manage their fears

SEE THE UNSEEN

To start a change, first lift up and see the possibilities. See beyond today. Make time to think, reflect, research, and explore, so you have a perspective beyond your current situation. Learn how others have done it. Research the market. Connect ideas from other situations and industries. Seek out a wise and innovative mentor. This access to new information opens up your mind to unseen possibilities. Your first thought may be, "I'm not a visionary." Most Wave Makers don't describe themselves as visionaries either, but they are curious, positive, and think beyond today. They don't let the "how" close off their ideas. They keep thinking, "What if we could..."

> "Do what you think is right. No one is going to give you the answer."
> —*Charley Johnson*

You may think that some people are just naturally creative or innovative and others aren't, but that isn't really true, according to researchers Jeff Dyer and Hal Gregersen in their book *Innovator's DNA: Mastering the Five Skills of Disrupting Innovators*. You learn to see what isn't there today by habitually asking the right questions: "Why?" "Why must it be that way?" "What if?" "What's the alternative?"

Let's look at Steve Jobs as the gold standard on seeing the unseen. Dyer and Gregersen note:

So what do we learn from Jobs's ability to think different? Well, first we see that his innovative ideas didn't spring fully formed from his head, as if they were a gift from the Idea Fairy. When we examine the origins of these ideas, we typically find that the catalyst was:

- a question that challenged the status quo
- an observation of a technology, company or customer
- an experience or experiment where he was trying out something new
- a conversation with someone who alerted him to an important piece of knowledge or opportunity.[1]

Jobs's questions and observation skills caused his perspective to change. This natural curiosity and openness to new information began the formation of new ideas. I found that most Wave Makers relied on this curiosity in approaching opportunities, problems, and exploration.

One Wave Maker, Charley Johnson, president of the Pay it Forward Foundation, shared his view on the importance of curiosity and learning: "Those crazy enough to think they can change the world are the ones who do. To have enough humility, but also that ego to believe you can do it. To be almost a walking contradiction. To just be unbelievably curious, to read so many different books, and listen to so many different opinions. To want to be taught something. To want to sit down with people smarter than you and that think differently than you and truly listen. I didn't do that in my last business. Things were going too well."

SEE THE OPPORTUNITY

Wave Makers see the upside and positive impact more than potential obstacles, problems, or risks. They talk about the importance of their change and the significant need. They are certainly aware of the challenges, but don't let it limit them.

Rich Sheridan, Wave Maker and CEO of software developer Menlo Innovations, started his wave long ago in his head. He fell in love with programming at the age of thirteen, in 1971. He was fascinated and knew, even at that age, that it was the future. Fast-forward twenty years and, in spite of his continued advancement and monetary rewards, he was very unhappy. Rich said, "I was working a lot of long hours. And it started to feel normal, which is scary. Nights, weekends, all-nighters from time to time. Our industry was known for working this way and I was part of it. So everything was 'normal' yet there was this nagging suspicion in the back of my head that wondered if I had picked the wrong profession. And another part of me said, 'there has got to be a better way to do this.'"

> **"I realized that the first thing I had to change was me."**
> —*Rich Sheridan*

Rich said, "I continued my journey of self-education. I'm searching, but, to be honest, I didn't really know what I was searching for. Yet I had confidence that 'I'll know it when I see it.'" And, he did: "For me it was reading a book called *Extreme Programming Explained* by Kent Beck, and I saw a Nightline video on Ideo, an industrial design firm. For the ABC News program, they redesigned a shopping cart in five days. It all clicked for me. I was a Vice President in 1999 and I decided, 'I'm going to build the best software team anywhere. And, I'll do it my way—not the way that everyone else does it.'"

This change in Rich's thought process started the transformation of Interface Systems, where Rich was VP of R&D. In less than two years, Rich's team at Interface Systems was transformed, then the internet bubble eventually shuttered Interface. Yet at this moment, Rich saw the entrepreneurial opportunity and founded Menlo Innovations relying on the same principles he learned at Interface Systems. Rich Sheridan and Menlo Innovations have been recognized by *Forbes, The Wall Street Journal,* NPR, and countless other media for their innovative approach to the workplace, and the company has been named one of Inc. 500's fastest-growing privately held firms in the United States.

During his team's remarkable transformation at Interface Systems, a team member approached Rich and asked why he had taken on such a big risk, one that could have easily failed. He saw the real risk differently: "I didn't risk anything in making the change. For me, the risk of not changing was much bigger."

For most Wave Makers, including Rich Sheridan, reaching their goal was their motivation and personal payoff. That ultimate benefit allowed them to look past the risks and challenges.

The Wave Makers I interviewed also had a very realistic view of problems, and they expected difficulties, so they weren't naive. Instead, they were confident in their ability to manage setbacks along the path to their goal. In fact, most *expected* resistance and obstacles, so setbacks didn't come as a surprise.

Overcoming obstacles takes a mind-set of embracing the challenge and feeling a sense of accomplishment when you reach your goal. This reminds me of one of my favorite movie scenes in *A League of Their Own*. Tom Hanks plays Jimmy Dugan, the coach of one of the first professional women's baseball teams during WWII. Geena Davis, as Dottie Hinson, wants to quit and go home because it's just too hard. With anger, Hanks responds, "It's supposed to be hard. If it wasn't hard, everyone would do it. The hard . . . is what makes it great."[2]

> "That's part of the charm! No one's ever quite done anything like this. Isn't it exciting that it would be hard!?!"
>
> —*Bruce Ballengee*

ASK, "WHAT CAN I DO?"

When there is a need or opportunity in front of you, you first must ask yourself this question: *What can I do? How can I make a difference?*

Wave Makers ask this question when they see a need, feel frustration, or experience disappointment. They quickly go to what they can do. Yet, the answer will be different for everyone. You aren't limited by your own skills and capabilities, because you can ask others to help. But begin by believing that you can contribute, make a difference, and start a change.

Wave Maker Guwan Jones, Corporate Director-Diversity Management, Workforce Planning & Human Resource Analytics of Baylor Health Care System, helped her leadership translate their commitment to diversity into a direct impact on the quality of patient care. She said, "There's always a cause and effect. I feel strongly that patients who aren't experiencing some likeness to their cultural background and to those things that are important to them are much less likely to pay attention to the advice we give them. And, when there are too many of the same, like-minded people in a room making decisions about patient care, it's not beneficial for patients. It makes us better when we have more than one opinion."

Guwan kept the bigger purpose in mind as she approached her change. When I asked her what made her take on this wave, she said:

> It was that I could put together diversity and workforce analytics, and impact the quality of patient care. And that hadn't really been done before. I wanted to figure out how to get it done. I kept hearing over and over from people that "You're just so transparent." And so I guess that has given me the latitude to ask questions and delve into things because I am very open. I'll share exactly what's on my mind and what I'm thinking. You know, I'm very honest. It may work out, it may not work out. But I really think there's something there and this is what I'd like to do. And, I've been given opportunities to just do that—to go find it and make it work.

She started with "What can I do?" and "How can I make a difference?"

Wave Makers, like Guwan, are practical optimists. They see the challenge and know the risks, but move forward with informed optimism. The opportunity and the impact of their change keep them going.

> "Be a realistic optimist. There aren't overnight successes on big changes. That's not how it works."
> —*Charley Johnson*

It's very unlikely that someone will come to you and say, "We need X, please." None of the Wave Makers I spoke with started this way. Even when the wave came to them because of a leadership request, it was always up to them to define how to make it happen. They individually saw the need and opportunity and found their role in realizing it.

Wave Makers don't wait for others to act or assume someone else will take on the change. Some Wave Makers see new possibilities or know the business needs to solve a problem. Others start a change because the opportunity is right there in front of them and they know they have to take it. Many take a relatively small first step without realizing that a much larger wave will follow.

Wave Maker Joe Nussbaum started The Big Event at Texas A&M University, the largest one-day, student-run service project in the nation, and the concept has expanded to seventy-five other universities. Nussbaum said, "I thought we should do some things to encourage more student service work. Ronald Reagan was in his second year of office and he had started a big initiative about volunteerism. It made us think, 'What can we do?'"

Joe said he woke up one night and it was clear what needed to be done. He explained, "We came up with the idea to have a large, coordinated effort to match up student groups with community organizations to create this huge service project on the same day. It started when we put together Reagan's request for volunteerism with what we could at A&M."

Like the change Joe and his fellow students began, waves ultimately start when a person motivated to action asks, "What can I do?" and "How can I make a difference?"

> "We presented the idea when no one was asking for it, but it was needed."
> —*Eric Buhrfeind*

KNOW WHAT YOU DON'T KNOW

It takes confidence to know what you don't know and ask for help. This isn't a reason to stop dreaming, but to acknowledge that it's unlikely you'll know everything you need to know. Waves aren't easy or they would have been done before. Wave Makers know what they need and ask for help through mentors, introductions, time, or assets. They think confidently about how others can help them realize their goals.

Mark Benton, a Wave Maker who redefined careers in research and development at PepsiCo, said, "I am never afraid to ask for help. I asked for help in tangible ways—people, friends, resources to give me knowledge and insights. I also ask for help from God. I knew I couldn't do it alone."

> "Accept that you don't have all of the wisdom that you need."
> —*Cynthia Young*

THINK PROGRESS, NOT PERFECTION

Focusing on forward movement rather than the ideal answer is where managing expectations come into play. You approach a change differently if you are looking for progress rather than the perfect solution or "the answer." Find the incremental success that moves you forward. It's not all or nothing. The Wave Makers I studied were most interested in progress, so they thought about change differently. They aimed for continuous movement toward the goal, not one big win. This allowed them to avoid the perfection trap and stay focused but patient.

> **"By design, we took dozens of baby steps forward."**
> —*Eric Buhrfeind*

Clint Hurdle, Wave Maker and manager of the Pittsburgh Pirates, said, "It takes courage to have patience. Change takes time—you *have* to be patient." You look for progress at each step, not the ideal all at once. That mind-set will change when and how you start.

TACKLE YOUR FEARS

There are challenges with any change, yet Wave Makers don't get bogged down by potential problems, barriers, or personal risks. They are most focused on the potential, the opportunity. Some of the Wave Makers I interviewed admitted to fears but weren't overtaken by them. They viewed their fears as a reality to be managed, not as a roadblock.

Or, as Wave Maker Lois Melbourne, former CEO of Aquire, said, "You have to take on risks if you want to start a wave."

WHAT KEEPS YOU FROM BEING A WAVE MAKER?

I'm not a psychologist, nor an expert on thought traps, but I know we all have them. Starting a change can bump right up against our deepest fears. Let's explore common reasons we get tripped up when starting a wave. In case you are feeling this is a little too close for comfort, I'll go first.

I can be a procrastinator and a perfectionist. I'm most comfortable when everyone is on the same page and in consensus. Growing up, I loved recognition and approval, and when I was in the corporate world, I was the one who left a great annual review thinking only about my one "development opportunity," not the successes or accomplishments. You get the idea. When I started my business, I had to face my fears of rejection and not having all the answers. Entrepreneurs learn very early in a special way that not everyone will be interested, buy your services, or agree with your recommendations. It took me time to internalize that this is the life of an entrepreneur, to embrace the challenge and not expect perfection. But I still have my setbacks, like everyone else.

You have your "go-to" fears and internal obstacles too. Let's identify them now so that you are prepared, because they will reappear in any wave.

Five common obstacles that keep us from being Wave Makers:

- **Fear** of being wrong, being inadequate, or hurting our standing
- **Lack of accountability**—the unspoken belief that someone else will do it
- **Assumptions** about what's important and what will work
- **Procrastination,** which delays action
- **Perfectionism,** which makes us feel we are never ready

Fear Draws a Line Between Beliefs and Actions

The word *fear* brings to mind a scary movie, skydiving, or public speaking, statistically one of the biggest fears. I am talking about a different kind of fear. It's the fear often hidden deep inside that makes us choose the status quo over a change we know is needed. In business, fear looks like:

- Not speaking up with an idea because you might look stupid
- Never asking for advice or help for fear that you won't look strong or in control
- Staying at the same company too long because the uncertainty of a new job is worse
- Not calling attention to yourself because it's safer to blend in
- Never admitting you don't know the answer
- Not offering a valuable recommendation that differs from your manager's view
- Avoiding new technology because you don't understand it

Fear draws a great big line between our beliefs about what is right, important, or needed and our *actual* actions. The goal of this section is to help identify your go-to fears so you are ready for them when they appear. As a high school student, Wave Maker Emma Scheffler started Insulin Angels to help children, and their families, after they are diagnosed with diabetes. When I asked Emma about her fears, she said, "My fear was, did anyone want this? Would the kids want to talk to me? At first, when I'd meet the kids at the hospital, I'd ask them to tell me their story and then I'd tell them mine. I decided I'd rather visit the hospital and maybe not help them, than not go and miss someone who really needed it."

Fear can keep us from showing any sign of weakness or vulnerability. Vulnerability isn't a word often used in business, but it's highly relevant because you are vulnerable when you step out and start a wave. Starting something new draws attention to you, and that can make you feel exposed.

I'm a fan of Brené Brown and her book *Daring Greatly,* which shares an insightful view on the transformative experience of vulnerability. Brown believes that vulnerability is the path toward conquering our fears and creating a real connection with others. These are two critical elements in starting and sustaining any wave.

Brown asserts that one of the underlying reasons for the fear of vulnerability is our scarcity culture—there is never enough to go around. We embody the scarcity culture by comparing ourselves with others, believing our change isn't important enough, or thinking that if others have a special quality then we don't. Goodness must be in limited supply.

In her research, Brown asked people to fill in the blank: *Never _____ enough.* Some of the responses were:

- Never good enough.
- Never perfect enough.
- Never powerful enough.
- Never successful enough.
- Never smart enough.
- Never certain enough.
- Never safe enough.
- Never extraordinary enough.[3]

What is your answer? The answer to this question will likely lead you to the very fears that will be the internal obstacles in starting your wave. This scarcity mind-set can drive fears like:

- I might be wrong
- I might lose my job
- I might be embarrassed
- I might not look as smart as the other leaders/speakers/participants/writers/ business owners
- I might not be appreciated

Fear also keeps us from doing what we clearly know how to do. Mike Boulanger, a hitting instructor for the Baltimore Orioles and previously the Texas Rangers, has worked with countless professional baseball players on not only how to improve their hitting but how to think about hitting. He works with players on staying focused on their actions (what's in their control) rather than anticipating the outcome, such as batting average or home runs. He believes that focusing on actions and tuning out distractions determines who makes it in the major leagues, where the pressure is intense and expectations stay high.

Boulanger said, "If you ask players if they can walk across a two-by-four board that is flat on the floor and be sure they won't fall off—they will quickly say, 'Yes!' Now, if you ask them if they can walk across that same two-by-four board that is thirty feet up in the air with thirty-five thousand screaming fans—there is a long pause. Some aren't sure. Then you add in all the thoughts in their heads—'It's on TV,' 'What will my Dad say?' 'If I screw up, will they send me back to AAA?' and it goes on. The consistently successful hitters just think about the bat and reacting. They tune out the rest. They trust themselves."

Most of us don't have to face thousands of screaming fans, but we do have to keep our go-to fears in check. The first step is calling out your fears when you start a wave. It helps to know the root cause so that you can create strategies to manage them. Determine whether your fear is based on the facts of your situation or hard-wired in the way you think.

If you fear that you lack the knowledge to start your change, then identify what is needed that you don't have. You can ask for help, partner with an expert, or research more about your idea. Decide if there is an action that will minimize your fear.

If your fear is just your favorite go-to fear, which appears regardless of the circumstances, then examine it a little more closely. Let's say that you fear losing your job because your deepest fear is tied to security. Step back and look at the facts: Is that a real fear based on likely events? Or is it a fear that you have carried since childhood and use as a silent crutch?

I spoke with an executive recently who admitted to this fear, which has kept her for far too long in a job that she no longer enjoys and that doesn't challenge her. Yet, she has been successful her entire career, is well respected, well connected, and has a wonderful résumé. There is a chance that a well-founded fear she had at eighteen is still alive and well at forty-five, even though the facts indicate that she is perfectly capable of succeeding in a new job.

Decide to tackle your fears. Wave Makers have fears and self-doubt at times, but it doesn't overtake them. They take action in spite of it.

> **"I wouldn't say I had real fears. It was getting to a new level in my career—where I was supposed to be. It was an evolution."**
> —*Kathy Korman Frey*

Wave Maker Allen Stephenson, creator of Southern Tide, shared the importance of how you think when going after your goals: "It's a mind-set that you will do it. You would never say something like, 'I didn't do it because someone said something to me,' or 'I never get around to it.' There is no 'would have.' There is no 'I didn't because.' You have to think, 'Hey, this is the one life I've got and this is where I'm going with it.' It doesn't matter whether you want to become a doctor, a professional football player, a construction worker—it doesn't make any difference. You have to give it your all."

What keeps you from having this "I can do it" mind-set? Identify your top three fears and at least one action you can take to minimize them.

1.
2.
3.

Embrace Fear

You have to face your fears and take risks to start a wave. The Wave Makers I spoke with took on everything from the fear of failing to the fear of losing relationships, and from the fear of being wrong to the fear of losing their financial security.

Yet, in many situations, fear can be a very positive force. It can:

- Be a sign that the change is important to you
- Indicate that you are learning
- Confirm that you are out of your comfort zone
- Give you creative energy
- Cause you to act on a priority

Find the positives of fear and don't aim to go around it or avoid it. If you embrace fear, it can work for you.

Wave Maker Jonathan Morris, who started open collaboration within the Young Presidents' Organization (YPO), said fear helped him act: "In YPO, when you reach a certain age, you leave the organization. We had just lost so much talent after winning the best chapter award. I went into my first two-day planning meeting as the new president very excited. I left terrified. We didn't know quite what we were doing yet, so we had to come up with a game plan. We had a big discussion on the real definition of success. In the past, success had been based more on competition, but we decided success needed to be based on how much we help other chapters."

While sharing and collaborating ran counter to their history, a new trend emerged. Jonathan said, "We decided that if we can get the YPO chapters working together and helping each other, it's going to make this a more valuable experience for our members. They're going to meet more people, hear about more things, and have more opportunities for learning."

> "We told everyone, if we trip, it will be over boulders,
> not over toothpicks."
>
> —Melisa Miller

Sometimes fear can act as a motivator. Charley Johnson, president of the Pay it Forward Foundation, shared how his fear caused him to take action:

> I had this house, this car, and business was going very well, but I wasn't happy. Day by day, month by month, things started to change for me. I started living for Fridays. For the first time in my career, I was looking forward to the weekend. I didn't have the energy I used to have to motivate me, much less others. For reasons I can't explain today, I decided to leave the business even though I don't like change and I really like security. A couple of months later, when the fear had subsided, that's when I decided to go for it. I decided I was going to commit to Pay it Forward 100 percent.

WORK THE ACCOUNTABILITY MUSCLE

Accountability is a necessary quality of anyone who starts a wave because the accountable act on their answers to "What can I do?" and "How can I help?" None of us shows equal amounts of accountability in all situations, but it is a muscle that we must get into the habit of using.

One of my mentors is a role model for accountability. She is an entrepreneur and has created very successful businesses through her own persistence and fortitude. As a result, when I have spoken with her about a disappointment or setback, her response has been very consistent and instructional: "Okay. So what are you going to do next?" or "So that didn't work, what other options are you considering?" She'd remind me to spend my energies on what I can influence instead of on factors outside my control. We all work on this from time to time, but it's a habit that some have engrained in the way they think.

I recently spoke to a leader on the accountability he feels in making his nonprofit a reality. He said, "What now drives me is the viability of the idea. And, candidly, I want all of the board members and everyone else involved to see the end result. That's really important. It's almost like going to Weight Watchers. Yes, I could try it on my own, but I'm not going to lose the weight. There's a certain amount of guilt that comes along with being in it with other people. I'm not going to show up and tell people that I didn't lose any weight because I ate too much pizza!"

Regardless of the internal motivation, the accountability muscle is essential for thinking like a Wave Maker and asking, "What can I do?"

Peter Block shares, in his book *Community: The Structure of Belonging,* a very interesting description of the difference between accountability and entitlement. Block says, "...taking responsibility for one's own part in creating the present situation is the critical act of courage and engagement.... This means that the essential aspect of the restoration of community is a context in which each citizen chooses to be accountable rather than entitled."[4]

Entitlement is an interesting and insightful counterbalance to accountability. At first, I associated *entitled* with the child who is never told no and always wants his way. But, when contrasted with accountability, the word *entitled* brings up another image. The entitled internally give their power away and believe that others will meet their needs, rather than taking personal responsibility. If the accountable take responsibility for their situation and their impact on the world, the entitled believe their needs will be met by the world around them. This is a very important distinction relative to being a Wave Maker, because changes take accountability and action.

> "I realized very early on that no one is coming to rescue me or give me a free pass. It's up to me."
>
> —*Tory Johnson*

Here are examples of an entitled mind-set, which will be an obstacle in life and most certainly in starting a wave:

- The professional frustrated with so much inefficiency at work, but who takes no action other than complaining to her friends about it
- The new entrepreneur who can't grow his business, yet isn't learning or trying anything new and remains frustrated
- The business leader who has a passion for analytics but isn't sure how to translate his ideas and, as a result, waits for more information
- The artist frustrated with his lack of recognition and success, yet who blames everyone and everything around him

This entitlement mind-set is based on a belief that the world, the organization, the manager, or the community will meet your needs and even that you deserve it. As Stephen Covey says in *The SPEED of Trust,* "We judge ourselves by our intentions and others by their behavior."[5] Even very successful or prominent people can become entitled. Entitlement is not based on age or circumstance, but on how you think. As my mom often told me, "If everything and everyone around you is wrong, you may be the one who needs to change."

> "I have a hard time with people complaining. Complain all you want—what are you going to do about it?"
>
> —*Charley Johnson*

As I shared in chapter 1, I first began thinking about accountability in such a personal way when my mother-in-law, Helen Johnson, passed away. She had many glorious moments but some major hardships too. Yet, throughout her life, in every situation, she always asked, "What can I do?" and "How can I help?" Good times or bad, she always went to those two questions. She was another role model for me on accountability.

> "One of my missions is to help others get out of their own way."
> —*Tory Johnson*

Wave Makers have this mind-set of personal responsibility and accountability when starting a wave, and in most other situations too. It's important to use the accountability muscle so it becomes a habit.

BEWARE OF ASSUMPTIONS THAT PREVENT ACTION

Assumptions limit us because they can become a reason not to take action. Do any of these sound familiar?

- "There's no use trying to change how we handle customer orders. We tried to change it two years ago and it was shut down."
- "The CEO has historically been squarely against any acquisitions. There's no point in researching this option no matter how good it looks."
- "There's no way I could start a business like this. I've been in a corporate role my entire career."
- "How could I start a Bible study group? Besides, there are others a lot more qualified to do it than me."
- "We really need to change this, but it's Marketing's responsibility not ours."
- "We need to do more to help the tornado victims, but I'm sure that others are in a much better position than me to help out."
- "I'd love to write a book, but a friend told me you have to get an agent and a publisher, and I have absolutely no connections in that world."

These are all assumptions. But if we treat them as facts without validation, they can give us a pass on any action, especially when they align with our deepest fears. If we have self-doubt and a fear of not being good enough, then starting a new business will increase our discomfort. The assumption that the move from a corporate role to entrepreneurship is too big saves us from exposing our uncertainty.

A recent graduate told me she could never recommend a new idea or influence her VP's strategy. She said she is viewed as too inexperienced and it was too soon. But, if she first asks the questions, "What can I do?" and "How can I make a difference?" she will find answers. Let's be realistic, it may be hard for her to start a big wave at first. But, where could she start if she had ideas to help the business? She could:

- Do some research and learn as much as possible about her topic to ensure she not only has an idea, but that it is credible
- Begin to share what she has learned with her colleagues and team
- Recommend a speaker or share articles aligned with her ideas
- Recommend a small experiment on a new idea
- Discuss her ideas with those who have more influence
- Identify others who care about the issue and discuss how to learn and work together

These actions may be more of a ripple than a wave, but if you assume that you aren't in a position to start anything, think again. Forget what's working against you and go back to "What can I do?" Start there.

FOUR ASSUMPTIONS THAT GET IN OUR WAY

An assumption is something we consider to be true or certain to happen, though we have no proof. It's not a fact, but we act as if it is. Like our fears, our favorite assumptions can create behaviors that become second nature.

Assumption #1: I Don't Know Enough

You can address the assumption that you don't know enough by learning everything you can about your topic. Remember how much information is at your fingertips. In chapter 4, "Trends and Your Waves" we'll look at how technology is leveling hierarchy and allowing us to directly access more information than ever before. Look to others who know more than you and learn from them. It's up to you.

Wave Makers gave examples of how they immersed themselves in the knowledge needed for their waves by:

- Joining groups (online and in person) of others with common interests
- Developing knowledgeable mentors and advisors
- Reading and engaging with experts
- Connecting with industry peers and colleagues interested in the topic

- Attending speaking events or webinars with direct access to experts
- Using YouTube and podcasts to learn
- Reading everything they could find on their topic

We all know that taking action to enhance our knowledge is important. The first steps are the hardest. These actions are rarely the "A" items on your to-do list or seem as important as the fire drills that overtake your day. Starting a wave takes commitment when no one is asking for it. The motivation has to come from within.

When I started PeopleResults, a change and organizational consulting firm, I asked dozens of people for information and advice, and I developed my go-to advisors. Some were paid and some were just friends and mentors. I had so much to learn about business structure and financials, marketing, social media, growing clients, and many other topics. I learned a lot on my own and through observation, but I also found experts who helped fill in my knowledge gaps quickly.

Accountable Wave Makers think about what they can learn, rather than assuming they don't know enough. If you have a wave in mind, it won't knock on your door. You have to decide to get smarter on your topic. The decision to learn more may well be your very first step. Incremental success begins with very small steps.

Assumption #2: It's Not My Job

When we think about the assumption "It's not my job," we picture the disinterested person who does the bare minimum at work. But think about this for a minute. We pride ourselves on being focused, on not taking on others' issues and problems so that we can be more productive and efficient. This works for the normal day-to-day activities, but waves don't follow organization charts. Start with the opportunity and the need, not who "owns it" or how it should get done. You'll likely need Idea Partners from other parts of the business, but don't confine your wave to your specific job.

Eric Buhrfeind, a Wave Maker who created the certification partnership between Accenture and MIT, didn't have global responsibility for training or learning. However, he influenced business leaders to consider such a program. He looked for the best answer and didn't limit himself to the confines of his role on the org chart.

> **"One little person with the right time and energy can absolutely start a change."**
>
> —*Fiona Grant*

Assumption #3: This May Not Work

The assumption that an idea may not work is an element of any change, because it hasn't been done before in quite this way. Call out your assumptions to determine whether they are real or just a mental roadblock that keeps you from taking action.

I spoke to a leader who changed the way her group approached building and growing client relationships. She admitted that she almost didn't get started because she had tried similar recommendations with her leadership twice before but got nowhere. She didn't have the needed support. Yet, she challenged her internal assumptions because her executive leadership had changed. It was worth another try. Her new approach worked, and she kept her old assumptions from shutting down her ideas.

Assumption #4: Someone Else Will Do It

The assumption that someone else will take responsibility is a classic reason for not taking action. We think: someone else will create a group to raise funds for the nearby disaster. Someone else will come up with the plans to make the product better. Someone else will develop new ideas for working together and reaching our goal. But, what if no one does? And what if you have ideas and options that no one else has? You assume that "someone" will do it—but what is keeping you from being that someone?

> "We're all powerful, and it's not that hard to make a request. Others will benefit—not just you."
>
> —*Fiona Grant*

PROCRASTINATION IS PRETEND RELIEF

Procrastination keeps us from a decision or action—at least today. Procrastination is pretend relief, as we delay the priority for yet another day. We usually don't procrastinate by sitting on the couch and doing nothing. We procrastinate by putting our attention on lesser priorities that give more immediate gratification. This is why we answer low-priority e-mails rather than spend time thinking about bigger—and more challenging—issues. E-mails are quick, and we get an immediate completion fix.

A wave is much bigger than a quick e-mail or an item on the to-do list. It doesn't happen overnight. If you are a professional procrastinator who needs the excitement of sliding in just before the deadline, you are in trouble with your wave. You can cram all night for the test or complete the presentation two hours before it's due when it's just up to you. Waves don't work that way. They take many people to build momentum and gain traction. Waves are bigger than just one person.

One of my waves was a badly needed workforce and talent program for a changing global organization. It was so big that I procrastinated getting started. I didn't quite know where to begin. There was no road map, no easy answer, and yet I felt the need growing day by day. I began to feel overwhelmed. Finally, I started thinking very small. I decided the actions I could take that week and identified the other people who cared about this issue too. I got started. My first week was the absolute hardest because no one was asking me for anything yet—but I knew they would. I had to carve out time to get started. Even though my first steps were small, I felt an incredible relief just by beginning the work.

PERFECTIONISM CRAVES THE IDEAL MORE THAN PROGRESS

Perfectionism is closely linked to procrastination, control, and desire for acceptance or approval of others. If you have these tendencies, be aware of them. Most perfectionists don't intend that their desire for quality become an obstacle. Perfectionism is a badge that many even wear with pride. The key is to know the difference between perfection and excellence, because waves require quick action before there is the perfectly defined solution.

I have seen—and have fallen into—perfectionism traps that get in the way of forward motion. For example:

- Waiting for the perfect time, though there will never be one
- Wanting to have a solution all figured out before beginning
- Feeling uncomfortable sharing an idea or intent without a well-thought-out plan
- Believing you have the perfect plan after hours of work and excluding other ideas as a result

If you have perfectionist tendencies, remember that starting a wave is about movement and progress, not one big successful event. Don't let perfectionism and the quest for the ideal solution keep you from going for it.

THE DNA OF WAVE MAKERS

In my research on those who start changes, I saw patterns not just in how they think or what they do, but in the way they approach life and work. I didn't want to miss this in *Make Waves*. I don't see the Wave Makers and others I interviewed as superhuman, but I saw in them particular behaviors and beliefs that make up who they are; these patterns help them when starting a wave, doing their work, or being a trusted family member or a friend.

I've outlined the four key elements of Wave Maker DNA that lay the foundation for the way they approach their lives and work overall—beyond a wave or change.

Figure 2–1: DNA of Wave Makers

Willingness to Look Beyond "Me"

Wave Makers place importance on reaching the goal more than on personal recognition. They are driven by the anticipated impact and change rather than personal accolades. This approach keeps them motivated even when setbacks or detours occur. In addition, they:

- **Believe their mission will benefit the greater good.** Wave Makers create momentum around an idea that reaches beyond self to make work, the community, or the world better. They are more focused on "what's in it for us" than "what's in it for me."
- **Make authentic relationships a top priority.** Wave Makers place a high priority on the meaningful and diverse relationships needed to achieve their goals. They are interested in being helpful to others. Relationships help them learn, build a strong network, and find meaning in their work.

Adaptable Persistence

Wave Makers have a healthy balance of persistence toward a goal while also adapting and adjusting when they get new information. Not deterred by setbacks, they are open to new ideas and insights. Wave Makers don't give up on the goal, but remain flexible on how it is accomplished. They also:

- **Believe in their idea and themselves.** Wave Makers believe in their ability to reach their goals in spite of obstacles. Grounded in their mission, they are both passionate about their idea and resourceful. They have a healthy confidence in realizing the goal without getting distracted or mired in future details.

Voracious Appetite for Learning

Wave Makers are always looking to enhance their knowledge and insights. Wave Makers seek out experts, read, listen, and build mentoring relationships. They are comfortable taking on a new idea or topic because they have confidence that they can learn what they need to know. Wave Makers:

- **Are comfortable with ambiguity; they find the way.** Guided by a strong belief in themselves and their goal, they have a bias for action and can move forward with a plan that has unknowns. They know when and how to seek expert advice for new insights as they move forward.
- **Are curious and ready to explore.** Wave Makers often ask, "Why?" and "What if?" It's in their nature to want to understand, apply new ideas to their work, and explore. Wave Makers examine topics that on the surface may not seem linked to their work, but they see connections.

Positive Collaboration

Wave Makers generally start from an intention of positivity and trust. They have a bias for transparency and authenticity in how they work with others. They aren't driven by ego as much as by a desire to work together toward a shared goal. In addition, they:

- **Engage and connect others to the mission.** Wave Makers know that the way they communicate with others is vital to advancing their idea. They know that it is important to share their goals with many people to ensure their idea's survival. They translate the meaning and purpose through stories that are relevant and meaningful to others.

As we discussed at the beginning of this chapter, *Make Waves* is dedicated to helping you start your wave and learn from others who have created change. Start off by looking at how you think and identify your go-to fears so that you can manage them. Any successful wave starts with the way we think.

THINK TIME

1. What is your answer to "I'm never _____enough"?
2. What are your most common go-to fears?
3. What caused you to have these fears?
4. How will these fears affect your ability to start your change?
5. How would you describe your risk tolerance?
6. In what situations are you most comfortable? What situations make you most risk averse?
7. How can you minimize the risk for your ideas or change?
8. In what situations do you demonstrate accountability in your thoughts and behaviors? In what situations do you find personal accountability most difficult?
9. What assumptions do you have that may affect your ability to see a needed change or the potential in your situation?
10. What goals do you have for changing the way you think so you are prepared to see the need or opportunity and act upon it?

PART 2

What You Know

Challenge conventional wisdom

- All important changes start at the top
- Change happens to us
- If I sell it, they will come
- Resistance can be seen
- The best way is the way we've always done it

Incorporate trends

Trends that affect what we want...

- Meaningful work
- Authenticity
- Short, fast and bite-sized
- Intense personalization
- Personal endorsements
- Human connection

Trends that affect how we work...

- Fading hierarchy
- Peer power
- Virtual reality
- Demographic tsunami

KNOW

CHAPTER 3

Conventional Wisdom About Change

While fear creates obstacles based on our view of ourselves, conventional wisdom creates obstacles based on our views of the environment. Both can keep us from taking action.

Let's look at conventional wisdom, which has its roots in the status quo, commonly held beliefs not always based on fact, and simplistic headlines. Conventional wisdom can run counter to the environment needed for a wave, so be on the lookout for it in your situation. It can consist of simple beliefs such as "Only senior leaders can sell to our customers," "They'll never hire a woman to work in that job," or "We want to avoid any negative comments online by our customers or employees."

"Conventional wisdom" is a term used to describe ideas or explanations that are generally accepted as truth by the public or by experts. It is so strong that it is assumed to be fact, without validation. The term is often credited to the economist John Kenneth Galbraith, who used it in his 1958 book, *The Affluent Society:* "The ease with which an idea is understood + the degree to which it helps one's personal wellbeing = Conventional Wisdom."[1] Let's deconstruct conventional wisdom. Galbraith's definition clearly states that it isn't based on facts or information. Also, consider the *ease* with which an idea is understood. If you take this phrase literally, we place a high value on our ability to easily grasp a topic or concept. Some people rely on conventional wisdom while considering complex issues with hundreds of interdependencies. The matter is deemed too complicated to fully understand and absorb, so conventional wisdom, which is already constructed, fits like a glove. It's easier that way. This is true for many political topics, business issues, and cultural differences that are complex and can't be organized easily into a yes/no list.

The second part of the definition concerns "the degree to which it helps one's personal wellbeing." So, this means that if the wisdom benefits us personally we are more likely to buy in to it. If it fits our priorities, our agenda, or our goals, conventional wisdom often goes unchallenged. This bumps right up against that innate resistance to change and an unspoken affection for the status quo. The ugly side of conventional wisdom is that it can perpetuate sexism, racism, and other prejudices.

Most environments have conventional wisdom at play, including the marketplace. Do the following statements sound familiar? "Customers will never buy one song at a time." "Social media is for kids." "People have to feel and touch merchandise before they buy it." Time makes this once-accepted wisdom sound uninformed and outdated.

Brett Hurt is a Wave Maker and an entrepreneur. He and his business partner, Brant Barton, founded Bazaarvoice so that retail customers could use technology to openly share comments about a company's products. Conventional wisdom was—and can still be—that you never want a negative comment to appear about your brand. This was especially true in 2005, when Bazaarvoice first started and social media was in its very early stages. Brett understood that we have had open sharing forever; it just wasn't supported by technology. He recalled a conversation with a recent client:

> He [the client] said, "Brett, you have to be kidding me. I'm going to let customers post anything about my products that I have in inventory— including one- and two-star reviews?" I said, "Well, don't you think that they've always shared that information? Does the movie theater control what you say about the movie to your friends? Does the author of a book control what you tell your wife and friends about it? Do you want to be at the front end of this information or on the back end of it? And, by the way, the biggest threat to you in the industry—Amazon—has been doing it since 1996. You have to take this leap of faith that your business won't tank if a product has one- to two-star reviews. They already talk about you; you just can't hear it today. Don't you want to know what they are saying? Don't you think that some of this talk is already reflected in your business metrics?"

Brett pushed back at the conventional wisdom that says it's best to hide bad news and discourage transparency between customers; but the absence of bad news isn't necessarily good news. It's better to know what your customers are saying about your business and your products.

Recently, I saw another great example of conventional wisdom that hampers an entire industry, in a story aired on CBS *Sunday Morning* A debt collection agency called CFS2, based in Tulsa, Oklahoma, pushed back at the conventional wisdom that the most successful debt collectors are those who exert the most pressure. CFS2, owned by Bill Bartmann, operates on the very different premise that people in debt don't have money, so browbeating them isn't going to help anyone.

Bartmann is trying something new. He doesn't hire the typical debt collector. Instead, he hires people with customer care experience. And he rewards them—not for how much money they bring in but for how many free services they provide. The goal is to assist those in debt to get back on their feet by being helpful. He said CFS2 will even assist customers in completing a job application or scheduling an interview. In a feature on CBS, Bartmann said, "Because if I can get you out of debt, you will have more money to pay me later." After a yearlong experiment, Bartmann says he is making 200 percent more than his competitors by challenging conventional wisdom. And his business is growing.[2]

We are all working with the same conventional wisdom when it comes to how change happens in organizations, the market, and communities. If taken seriously, these pieces of "wisdom" may keep you from ever seeing the opportunity, much less getting started.

The conventional wisdom examples here also relate to the assumptions we reviewed in the previous chapter. Let's see if any of these affect how you look at your role, your likelihood of success, or how you answer the question "What can I do?"

IMPORTANT CHANGES START AT THE TOP

If you believe that all significant changes come from the top, then you likely believe that those with big titles must have the answers. Of course, in larger organizations, top leaders start changes as they set the vision and strategy. But they aren't the only ones who can. If you unwind that strategy, where did it begin? Who influenced it? How will it become a reality? What is needed from you and others? And top leaders can't have all of the answers, even when they have a compelling vision and strategy. It's just not possible. They need others to ask themselves, "What can I do?" "How can I make a difference?" or "What if?" A strategy has many threads, so there are plenty of opportunities to be a leader of change, regardless of your job title.

There are countless familiar examples of how one person took action that started a big change. Consider Bill James's impact on baseball through the introduction of sabermetrics, an empirical analysis of baseball. Sabermetrics was invented in 1976 when James, an economics major and baseball fanatic, was working as a night watchman in Kansas. As a complete baseball outsider, he began to test the assumptions baseball clubs had been using for over a hundred years to see if they stood up to modern statistical analysis.

James started self-publishing his conclusions, long before it was a trend to do so, and his methods took hold with other baseball fans interested in statistical analysis. The movement grew, completely outside of traditional baseball—the baseball executives, scouts, broadcasters, and commentators. How could a group of people who had never played the game know anything about how baseball is really played, much less be experts?

The first major league baseball team to use sabermetrics to make player and strategy decisions was the 2002 Oakland Athletics. The story was told in *Moneyball,* by Michael Lewis,[3] and in the movie by the same name. While the movie focused on Billy Beane, the general manager, the real story began with a young person with self-acquired knowledge and the ability to see something others didn't.

General manager Billy Beane had only $40 million to spend on players, yet he had to compete against big-market teams spending $200 million. James's wave informed the thinking behind Beane's assistant GM, Paul DePodesta, a Harvard-educated sabermetrics expert who had never played the game either. Following Bill James's road map, DePodesta created a sabermetric profile that showed proven ability based on metrics that would be undervalued by those in traditional baseball. The Oakland Athletics went on to win the American League West that year in spite of losing three of their best players.

Bill James started the wave that transformed baseball though he had no authority, no official role, and had never played the game.

Lindsay Pender, a Wave Maker and a nurse with six years' experience, influenced the change in neonatal ICU policies at her new, smaller hospital because she brought knowledge from the hospital where she'd previously worked, which boasted a nationally known advanced care unit. The change happened because she was committed to helping babies in the neonatal ICU.

> "It probably took about nine months from when I first started trying to getting everyone involved, the tests and the approvals. It took time, but we got there."
>
> —*Lindsay Pender*

Some changes definitely need visible leadership support because of the scale and impact. But a change doesn't have to start at the top.

It can be easy to think, "I'm not in a position to change anything. What can I do?" There are many examples of people who started their own wave because they were able to set aside the conventional wisdom that changes must start at the top or from someone with a certain title.

CHANGE HAPPENS TO US

The myth that change happens *to* us is heavily dependent upon our view of accountability and on what's within our control. We can face a job loss, a transfer, or an illness that changes everything. These changes are significant, and it may seem that you have no ability to influence them. Yet there are still choices.

Wave Maker Emma Scheffler's change, creating Insulin Angels to help families and children first diagnosed with diabetes, arose out of her own disappointment. Emma was a high school soccer player, and she had hopes of playing in college someday. She and her family received lots of medical information, yet they were uncertain what her diabetes diagnosis meant for her dreams and her life.

Emma had many long car rides to soccer practice with her dad, Leon Scheffler. They talked about how to turn her experience into a positive. Her dad asked her a question that started her journey. He said, "What would have made it easier for you?" Emma answered, "It would have helped me so much to have talked to someone who was like me and closer to my age—someone who had been through it."

> "On the way to soccer practice and games we'd talk about what we could do to have some positive benefit from this, but we didn't know what it was yet."
>
> —*Emma Scheffler*

Those conversations on the way to soccer began the search to find the good in disappointment. Emma flipped the idea that change happens to us and got to "What can I do?"

Change feels different when we decide rather than allowing others to decide for us—even if we wanted the same thing all along. A friend had been very unhappy in her job for some time. She wanted to leave but hadn't yet decided how and when. She even considered resigning without her next job in place. Yet one day I received a tearful phone call from her telling me that her company had eliminated her position, though she had received a competitive severance package.

As I listened, I wondered why she wasn't overjoyed. She had been given a wonderful exit strategy complete with a nice financial transition that would give her time to find a new job. I asked her why she was upset, when she had already decided to leave and had been so unhappy. She said, "Because *I* wanted to decide when I was ready."

I've been part of many conversations just like that one, and I've felt that way too. We like to feel we are in control of our destiny—whether we are or not. Even limited control or influence over change is essential. And looking for ways to take action is one way to have that influence in our life..

A wave requires moving past the myth that change only happens to us and quickly to "What can I do?"

IF I SELL IT, THEY WILL COME

This belief implies that a dazzling presentation or sales pitch will win the day. There is so much emphasis on selling, convincing, and persuading today. Look at the number of books dedicated to getting the pitch right. The problem comes with the belief that an incredible presentation is enough to engage others in a lasting change.

Here are a few recent examples of great presentations and sales efforts that didn't achieve the desired result:

- A consultant gave an impressive, well-rehearsed presentation to a potential client. He shared relevant examples of his team's capability, along with a creative marketing brochure. He won the work but did little to confirm expectations, build a relationship, or agree how to deliver the work. At first, he thought his great sales presentation was his big hurdle, but he soon realized that he hadn't built a foundation for longer-term success. He finished the work, but hadn't achieved his original goal of becoming a long-term trusted partner for this client's change.

- A senior leader was in charge of major organizational changes. She spent days tinkering with her script and slides for the big meeting and had prepared stories to illustrate the importance of the change. Her direct reports applauded her flawless presentation at the company-wide meeting. It was a great presentation, but she had no real commitment for the change from the larger organization, though she assumed otherwise. She was too focused on the big performance and missed the individual and smaller conversations critical to engaging others, finding meaning, and building commitment.

- A new graduate had a wonderful college résumé and impressed his new employer with his confident interview. He had done his homework before he joined and knew all of the manager's titles and roles. He made a great first impression, but he spent his first year more focused on impressing others than delivering great work. He thought all it took was a great performance, so he missed opportunities to make a substantive contribution.

- An entrepreneur was eager to grow her business. An essential early step was convincing a well-known local retail store to carry her new jewelry line. She took samples to her meeting with the store's manager and she rehearsed her script to perfection. The owner was polite and appeared interested, but never called back to place an order. The entrepreneur learned later that, while her presentation was great, she hadn't listened to the owner's feedback about the type of merchandise she wanted to carry and the prices she wanted to offer. This entrepreneur missed a significant boost to her business by concentrating on her own performance rather than listening and adapting.

Guwan Jones, a Wave Maker who has worked to make diversity of caregivers a part of patient care, described the importance of individual conversations over presentations: "The best way to get people on board is by making them feel like they have a piece in it. Helping them have an opportunity to respond to me one on one and meeting individually helps do that. I'm talking to them and saying, 'You know, I'm new to this work, so I'm here to understand. Here's what I'm thinking. How does that feel? What does that look like?'" She didn't rely on a big presentation because she was also listening and learning what could work.

A wave isn't about a one-time performance. It takes involving others, conversations, flexibility, and adaptability. One presentation will never be enough, even though presentations will likely be needed at times to share information with large groups. If you enjoy the stage, remember also the informal and one-on-one conversations essential to successful and lasting change.

Wave Maker Trisha Murphy Rae, co-founder of Christmas is for Children, has built up a committed network of volunteers who believe in the cause. If you watch Trisha, you learn that she can command the room with her passion and enthusiasm for helping families in need. She couples that enthusiasm with tremendous attention to relationships. Trisha shows appreciation by hosting thank-you lunches for volunteers, a brunch at her home to recognize the mothers in her community, and get-togethers to discuss future plans, all in the name of conversation and fun. If you frequent the neighborhood Starbucks, there's a good chance you'll see Trisha having coffee with a volunteer or supporter. She relies on informal relationships and discussions as well as the formal presentations.

CHANGE IS A STEP-BY-STEP PROCESS

When you've finished reading *Make Waves*, I hope it's clear that change isn't purely sequential or a matter of simply following a detailed project plan. I have been in dozens of business meetings to discuss upcoming strategic changes, and the most common next step is the introduction of key milestones and the project plan. I'm not suggesting that a plan isn't important, because I absolutely love a good project plan. But if you have your sights on a wave, it's what happens around the edges of a project plan that builds commitment and momentum.

In chapter 6, we'll explore how waves happen organically and require incremental planning with ongoing adjustments. Change is propelled by the decisions of human beings, and we are anything but orderly, sequential, and predictable.

Your investor needs more time. Your collaborator has a great addition at the last minute. Your product has a flaw that will affect your success, so you have to redo it. The leadership sponsor behind your idea just resigned. The best plans can't anticipate everything that will happen or all you will learn along the way.

Mark Benton, a Wave Maker who developed a new approach to careers in PepsiCo R&D, described how his wave changed as it grew: "From my background in leading change, I knew the big steps to take. In a change like this, you don't always know Step A, B, and C all the way to the end. At first, I didn't know how big it was going to be. What we've been able to accomplish looks totally different from where I thought we were going to go. So we had to be flexible and evolve."

A detailed or complex plan doesn't guarantee successful change. A plan can address about 60 percent of the issues—those that are predictable. If you plan incrementally and adapt as you go, then it may address up to 75 percent of them. But you will still have surprises and changes if you listen and adapt. A wave takes on the energy of the human element, which cannot be fully represented in a project plan.

> "We were both specific and flexible. We had to be."
> —*Melisa Miller*

While a professor at The George Washington University, Wave Maker Kathy Korman Frey created the Hot Mommas® Project, the largest crowdsourced library of women's stories together with teaching tools for use in home and work settings. Her wave didn't start with a clearly defined two-year plan; it grew organically and evolved over time. I asked Kathy if she always planned to be a leading voice in the growth and advancement of women. She answered, "At the time this began I had a consulting company and I was doing well financially, and I had no plans to change direction. I had gone to Harvard Business School and I came from a niche consulting firm before that. My brain was a spreadsheet. I'd done valuations of companies and I'd been focused on maximizing value. I wrote business plans and did executive planning sessions. It absolutely never occurred to me that I'd get into the women's education and leadership arena."

Yet women kept asking Kathy about her success as a woman and how she was making her life work personally. After she gave a presentation or taught a class, young women wanted to know Kathy's personal story along with her more visible career history. Her wave appeared and emerged over time. She added, "I'm big on gut instinct. It doesn't happen all of the time for me, but when I have it, it will be very strong. And, this was one of those times. The Hot Mommas® Project had almost a gravitational pull for me. Doors just opened that were never opened to me before. Up to that point, with my background, I thought success was about financial success. But the Hot Mommas® Project completely inspired me."

Revisit your assumptions about the orderliness and predictability of a change, so that you can both adapt your own style and have the right up-front expectations.

RESISTANCE CAN BE SEEN

What you see isn't always what you get. How many times have you heard the response to "How did it go?" be "I think everyone is on board. I didn't hear any big objections." I was on a call recently when the leader said, "I'll take silence as agreement." Of course, on the more routine topics that is an efficient way to run a meeting. Yet in a wave you are looking for commitment and an enthusiastic "I'm in and here are my ideas"—not "I didn't find a reason to openly disagree with you."

> **"Figure out where your resistance is coming from and why. Then, see if you can solve for those things one at a time."**
> —*Kate Rogers*

In chapter 5, we'll talk more about the value of conflict and disagreement. Many Wave Makers said that some conflict helped them decide what would work by bringing concerns out in the open. But what about resistance below the surface? Here are subtle clues that you may have unseen resistance on your hands:

- Silence on an important and meaningful topic
- Change in behavior (e.g., a typically engaged or outspoken person who is silent)
- Comments or questions that reinforce the status quo
- An overly emotional reaction, even if not directed to you or the topic
- Consistent unavailability for a discussion after repeated tries
- Failure to follow through on committed actions in spite of consistent agreement to do so

These examples aren't as direct as "I have concerns" or "I know you have some good ideas, but I'm not comfortable moving forward right now"—that is productive resistance you can address. But some resistance is never spoken, so you have to look for clues.

Resistance is typically caused by a divergence from:

- **Beliefs**: "What you are saying doesn't align with what I believe to be true"
- **Feelings**: "These changes make me feel uncertain or afraid"
- **Values**: "This goes against my personal values"
- **Trust**: "I don't trust you as a credible voice on this topic"
- **Actions**: "Your actions don't give me confidence"

In my research, I found that the most common initial resistance occurred under the surface. Examples included:

Beliefs—*an investor who gave positive signals but privately didn't believe the business case was accurate*

Feelings—*team members afraid to give up individual perks and change the way they develop software*

Values—*a leader who didn't believe in sharing the profits with anyone other than senior leaders*

Trust—*colleagues who didn't initially trust someone less experienced, even though she had more knowledge*

Actions—*the group leader who preferred to compete with other groups rather than collaborate*

In all these cases, the wave was successful in spite of initial passive resistance because the Wave Maker overcame it through close collaboration and communication. But, it's hard to break down resistance if you miss that it even exists.

Tips for addressing resistance:

- **Listen.** Resistance can simply be a need to be heard. Start with understanding someone else's point of view.
- **Understand the root cause.** Consider why the resistance is there, so that you know what to do with it. Is it the topic, the way it was shared, or the person who shared it? Explore why the resistance exists.
- **Educate.** Persuasive new information is needed before you can overcome resistance and update conventional wisdom. Identify needed information based on the root cause of the resistance.
- **Translate.** Share useful information in a way that is relevant for that person or group. Telling a story or an analogy can be a way to take new information and apply it.

- **Work together.** Find the common ground that you can stand on going forward. Identify an issue that can bring you together. For example, Wave Maker Guwan Jones's closing comment—"Let's work together on this"—strikes a positive and collaborative tone.

Don't be too comfortable with "no news is good news"—look more closely for signs of resistance. There may be subtle signals that the unspoken needs your attention.

THE WAY WE'VE ALWAYS DONE IT IS BEST

The mother of all conventional wisdom is the belief that no matter how great the idea, it can never overtake the way we have always done things. This conventional wisdom is more prevalent in some organizations and communities than others. But it can be alive and well even if not openly spoken in quite this way. After all, the "way we've always done it" is predictable, and everyone knows what to expect. It seems easier because it is known and doesn't require the energy that trying something new does.

Wave Maker Bruce Ballengee challenged conventional wisdom when he created Pariveda Solutions. He wanted all employees to have meaningful financial incentives, not just the senior leadership. His goal was to enable rapid advancement and growth, rather than create obstacles to prevent it. He changed the way the organization approached selling and building client relationships, and made compensation completely transparent. Bruce explained that it can be a big change when someone with a great deal of previous experience joins Pariveda Solutions because so much of the conventional wisdom associated with consulting work and organizational ground rules have to be set aside to operate in the Pariveda culture.

By design, a wave bumps up against "the way we've always done it." There can be great power in the status quo. I spoke to some who tried to start their change but felt that they couldn't get beyond the way things had always been done. The history and culture felt overpowering.

The best way to address "how it's always been done" is by finding even a small success that begins to test that belief.

Mike Williams, vice president of Human Resources at Trinity Industries, shared a wonderful example that pushed on the status quo. You see, Trinity has many facilities in small towns, and the search for quality welders had been ongoing. Mike and his team were actively discussing how to attract and grow talent in smaller markets where special skills are needed.

One day Mike was touring a Trinity facility and he had an epiphany. The plant manager introduced Mike, to one of their best welders, a woman named Emily. Mike recalled, "I stopped and said, 'Wait a minute. I want to talk with Emily.' I asked her why she liked her job. She told me that she had been a single mom working two jobs and living with her mom. She said that Trinity advertised a job that would teach her a skill [welding]. And, she had the ability to be at home at night and on weekends. She told me she had since made enough money to find a place of her own for herself and her kids."

Mike left that day having seen a new pipeline for talent, one that he and the plant manager stumbled upon. Mike said, "Trinity had advertised for people who wanted to learn to weld, and, luckily, Emily applied. Welding is immediately assumed to be for men, but it didn't have to be."

Women were a completely untapped talent resource for Trinity. Mike Williams and his HR team set in motion a series of changes encouraging women to consider a career in welding. And they had a great example in Emily. But the change only happened because Mike recognized an opportunity after one small success and then connected it to a critical business need.

Julie Porter, Wave Maker and founder of Front Porch Marketing, bumps up against "the way we've always done it" when she works with her clients on social media. She faces comments like, "Social media isn't important," "We don't want our employees sharing openly," and "Let's get a new intern to handle our social media." She tries to influence her clients with new ideas based on today's needs and tomorrow's trends rather than on history: "One of the things that I love about social media is that it's changing every day. You have to be current. Watch and listen to what others are talking about, including leaders inside and outside the industry. The successes will be small at first, but you have to stay with it and you'll see untold benefits. But you have to get over yourself and the way you've always done it."

THINK TIME

1. What conventional wisdom exists around me that may affect my wave?
2. How is conventional wisdom working for me or against me on my change?
3. What strategies can I use to push against conventional wisdom?

For each conventional wisdom identify the impact and applicability to your personal readiness and to the readiness of your organization or broader community.

Myth	My belief	My organization or community's view	Impact on me and my wave
1. Important changes start at the top.			
2. Change happens to us.			
3. If I sell it, they will come.			
4. Change is a step-by-step process.			
5. Resistance is visible.			
6. The way we've always done it is best.			

CHAPTER 4

Trends and Your Wave

Make Waves is about turning your idea for change into a reality. Your timing couldn't be better, as the world around us is cooperating with new technology and a transformation of the social community. There are many new opportunities for starting your wave, given fundamental changes in the way we think, interact, and work. Each of you will have a different level of experience and knowledge of these trends, but that's okay—we will look at them together in a new way based on their likely impact on your change. So, even if the topic is familiar, this chapter is designed to give you the opportunity to explore trends through the lens of change and give you new insights.

Makes Waves is not focused primarily on trends, yet I believe that these key trends will affect the way you approach your wave. If you have an idea for a new service or see an opportunity for making your organization better, you have the wind at your back. Today, there are new and growing ways to connect with others, engage, and get involved that didn't even exist just a few years ago. These forces are leveling the playing field, and there are new technologies to help you get started.

Let's take a step back and look at some relevant trends that may change your perspective on your wave. We'll examine trends from two perspectives:

- Trends that affect what we want
- Trends that affect how we work with others

TRENDS THAT AFFECT WHAT WE WANT

There are emerging trends on what individuals want today and in the future. They will likely affect the way you develop your ideas, share them, and collaborate with others on your wave.

Meaningful Work

There is much written today about finding happiness. The premise underlying much of the literature is that finding what makes you happy will make your life complete and satisfying. In fact, there are more than 115,000 books on how to find happiness, be happier, and stop doing what doesn't make you happy. Of course, we all aspire to be happy, but research tells us there is more. A recent study from the *Journal of Positive Psychology* stated that "Happiness without meaning characterizes a relatively shallow, self-absorbed, or even selfish life, in which things go well, needs and desires are easily satisfied, and difficult or taxing entanglements are avoided." The focus was more on "me" than on "we."[1]

In Adam Grant's book *Give and Take,* his research contrasted the values of takers and givers. Respondents had to choose between the following:

List 1:

- Wealth (money, material possessions)
- Power (dominance, control over others)
- Pleasure (enjoying life)
- Winning (doing better than others)

List 2:

- Helpfulness (working for the well-being of others)
- Responsibility (being dependable)
- Social justice (caring for the disadvantaged)
- Compassion (responding to the needs of others)

According to Grant, "Takers favor list 1, whereas givers prioritize the values in List 2."[2] The givers place more importance on meaning and a life of value.

Meaning is defined as an orientation to something bigger than self. In my research with Wave Makers, I found that they are motivated to achieve goals beyond their own personal success. Meaning and purpose are key factors in not only their personal motivation, but in building a lasting commitment to change—not just compliance. They know their "why" and use it to keep others involved and committed too. They have a passion for their change.

Guwan Jones, the Wave Maker who connected diversity to patient care, shared how she developed a passion for her work and cause:

> While I was in school working on my bachelor's, the world was facing HIV and AIDS. And I wanted to take care of those folks. At first, I went to school to become a physician. I worked in a clinic and found out that I really want to help people, but I also want to have kids and more control of my life. I didn't want to live off of a pager. I learned that there are a lot of different ways that you can take care of people. So, seeing people diagnosed with HIV or AIDS and having a really hard time made me

see the broader community out there. It's also part of the community I live in. I'm African American and African Americans are suffering from these diseases in a higher proportion than the rest of the population. I felt a need to help with the prevention and spread of this disease and others. And so, a lot of what I do I think is selfish. It is fulfilling something that deep down I need to fulfill.

Guwan is fulfilling this purpose not by being a physician involved in direct patient care but by her commitment to translating diversity and workforce analytics so that patients ultimately connect with caregivers like them. She kept her passion for quality patient care and made it core to her work, regardless of her position.

There is also a generational dynamic at play regarding the search for meaning in work. Millennials have grown up believing community service is a core responsibility rather than an extra. A 2010 Pew Research Center study found that millennials place a higher priority on helping people in need (21 percent) than having a high-paying career (15 percent).[3] Many baby boomers grew up feeling that not only did they want the high-paying career, they were willing to wait for it. The promise of good things to come was a successful motivator.

But even baby boomers are rethinking career and the meaning of work. They are living longer and working longer as a result, and the trend is toward second or encore careers that combine a personal passion with paid work. According to the nonprofit group Encore.org, as many as nine million people aged forty-four to seventy are now doing work that combines their personal passion with a social purpose. An additional thirty-one million are interested in making the leap into more meaningful "encore careers."[4] Meaning isn't the exclusive right of one generation. We all have this goal deep down inside, even if we lose track of it.

In his search for meaning, Rich Sheridan, CEO of Menlo Innovations, changed the course of his career and his life. Rich said, "We all seek purpose. I think we are, by and large, wired as individuals and as communities to leave the world a better place than we found it. I know it's hard and the world is conspiring against me, but that's my intent. These days, particularly, since the world is so complex, we have to do it in concert with others. There are very few individual heroes anymore."

After much learning and searching, Rich had ideas for a big change at the software company where he'd been working. He began asking the developers on the team he was leading to work in pairs, partner with sponsors, and leave their offices and cubicles behind in favor of an open-room environment that had formerly been a factory. The developers were asked to deliver working software every two weeks, which was a dramatically condensed timeframe from industry standards. His team was skeptical at first, but believed in the change after they experienced the difference firsthand. The results surpassed Rich's own expectations, and he took what he learned as a VP of R&D and cofounded Menlo Innovations, with one focused purpose: *Ending human suffering in the world as it relates to technology.*™ That's another way of saying that technology should be simple, responsive, and easy to use rather than a painful obstacle.

> "Human beings are wired to work on something bigger than themselves."
> —*Rich Sheridan*

Some Wave Makers help others fulfill their potential by adding meaning to their work and their lives. Bruce Ballengee, Wave Maker and CEO of Pariveda Solutions, touched on this point: "What does it take for a person to completely fulfill their potential? It means that at some point in their life, they're going to want to be about helping other people, because that is what brings fulfillment. You can't help yourself without helping other people. It's becoming a trusted advisor, having a network of people that trust you, and being engaged in serving your community. All of these come together in a servant leader."

What does this trend toward more meaning in work and life mean for your change? In chapter 7, we'll look closely at how successful changes must appeal to a larger meaning and purpose. We only commit when we see the bigger value. This trend indicates that meaning will likely become even more important as the workforce composition changes and careers last longer.

Wave Maker Emma Scheffler, a high school student and the creator of Insulin Angels, described how she knew her work mattered: "When we first started, we met with a mother who already had two other family members in the hospital going through major illnesses when her daughter was diagnosed with diabetes. You could tell she was very worried when we met her. I went in and sat down to talk with the little girl with diabetes. She looked up and asked me, 'Did your mom cry too when you were diagnosed?' I said 'Yes, she did.' And I knew right then that we were doing something very important."

There can be meaning in even a conversation about small things. Your wave doesn't have to change the world or put you on *Time* magazine's "Most Influential" list. Meaning can be creating beautiful products, a positive work environment, or new opportunities for those you care about. Know what is meaningful to you and remember it when you share your ideas with others.

Remember the trend toward meaningful work when planning your wave:

- Know your "why."
- While there will be actions and plans, always return to why your wave matters.

- In any communication, keep the meaning visible. Say it, say it again, and then say it again.
- Give yourself encouragement when you hit obstacles and remember to take joy in the small steps forward.

Authenticity and the Real Deal

The search for authenticity is based on a growing expectation of honesty and transparency. In our social world, where much more is shared and discoverable, it is expected that who you are and who you say you are align. "Authentic" is one of the most common words used today in the business, leadership, and self-development arenas. In our over-advertised, Photoshopped, create-your-brand world, we search for the real deal. Authenticity—the truthfulness of origins, attributions, commitments, sincerity, devotion, and intentions—stands out.

Best-selling author and marketing guru Seth Godin takes authenticity one step further, saying, "If it acts like a duck (all the time), it's a duck. Doesn't matter if the duck thinks it's a dog, it's still a duck as far as the rest of us are concerned. Authenticity, for me, is doing what you promise, not 'being who you are.'"[5] He connects being who you are with what you actually *do*.

We know that trust is based on the principles of honesty, openness, integrity, and authenticity. We will learn that trust matters in growing an interested group around your change. Authenticity indicates that your words and actions align, which we know is critical to a trusting relationship. Wave Maker Clint Hurdle, manager of the Pittsburgh Pirates, explains that a desire for trusting relationships and alignment in words and actions isn't new:

> The truth is, baseball players are no different today than they were thirty years ago when I played the game. Sure, how they use technology is different and the world has changed, but as human beings they are no different. They are motivated by the same things today that the players were motivated by back then. First, players have to trust you before they let you coach them. They have to believe you have their best interests in mind. Second, they have to believe that you can help them get better. If they trust you, then they will let you coach them. Finally, they have to know that you care about them and know what is going on in their lives and with their families. They want to be more than a fast left-hander. They are important as a human being and they want to know that they are important to you and the team.

Authenticity is based on choices we make every day. We decide if we will be real and let ourselves be seen and heard. Authenticity is essential in building and growing your wave. Many Wave Makers have very targeted and limited reliance on formal channels. Their momentum results from discussions with small groups, one-on-one conversations, and back-of-the-napkin collaborations that rely on trust. Big meetings are helpful for sharing information, but the smaller, informal conversations build partnerships and a community around the change. These small conversations require an honesty and transparency built on a trusting relationship.

> "In my mind, almost everything goes back to relationships, credibility, and authenticity."
>
> —*Cynthia Young*

Here are some ways you can show authenticity and convey the "real deal" in your change:

- Be transparent about the value, but also the realities, of making the change. Don't oversell or sugar coat.
- Develop advocates for your change who care about the cause and are trusted by others.
- Avoid slick or packaged communications more like advertising than a genuine appeal.
- Show vulnerability by indicating that you don't know everything and value others' ideas.
- Share your ideas and plans in real and simple language. We'll look more at the importance of simple language in chapter 5.

Fast and Bite-Sized

Anyone can create a video that is shared around the world in minutes. And a few seconds of a video is all we need. Social media connects people in distant places on any topic, instantaneously. We tell social media friends to join us at the game in a quick post from our phone. We advise our followers in a few words to avoid a traffic jam, and we share pictures of everything and everyone. There are many fast ways to tell our friends, "Here's what I think, what I'm doing, and what you should know."

If one person knows something, we all can. We can get the news from one another through social media much faster than from any news program. Bombarded with information, we no longer expect to wait. We want it now and we want to be part of it.

Speed also means that we need our information to be short and to the point. There is growing evidence that social media and changing technology are rewiring our brains so that we have shorter attention spans than ever before. Statistic Brain, research provider to business and media, reports that the average attention span in 2012 was eight seconds, down 33 percent from the 2000 average.[6]

We even like bite-sized nuggets better. According to KISSmetrics, shorter posts aren't just for Twitter. Facebook posts of fewer than 250 characters receive 60 percent more engagement than lengthier posts. And you'll get up to 66 percent more engagement if you cut them down to fewer than eighty characters.[7] We are more hurried than ever, and in most situations short is no longer seen as lacking substance but rather as an asset.

> "Don't put all the dessert on the table at once. Bring a few things out at a time. Then, test it and make sure it works. As your changes have uptake, then introduce something else new. Pace yourself."
>
> —*Mark Benton*

Hyperconnected individuals are increasing the trend for short and fast. They are almost always connected by mobile technology and tend to use multiple sources simultaneously—they are online, texting, checking social media, posting photos, and keeping up with Twitter simultaneously, even when on the go. This way of working and engaging has become the norm in business today.

Our mobile society is always connected, and it doesn't matter where we are currently located—we can participate from anywhere. And the trend toward mobile is exploding as consumers have come to expect to be engaged all of the time. Mobile is also blurring the lines between work and personal time. Not only can we work anytime from anywhere, but multitasking has become an art form.

Glenn Engler, CEO of Digital Influence Group, calls needed bits of information "snackable content"—bite-sized chunks of material that can be quickly "consumed" by an audience.[8] Social media is based on bite-sized information, and our increased multitasking drives the need for just the headlines. This short and quick, sample mentality is a trend in nearly every facet of modern life. Snackable content doesn't replace our need for depth, however. We just want to dive deeper only when we choose. Otherwise, the headlines will do.

The trend toward bite-sized nuggets also drives engagement. Engler says, "It drives trial—and, as a parallel, engagement. It's easy to nibble and try without feeling that it's too much effort or the impact will be too negative."[9] His point of sampling a new idea reinforces the importance of experimentation, which we'll explore further in chapter 6.

Wave Maker Joe Nussbaum started The Big Event, a student-run service project, at Texas A&M University. In the first year, Nussbaum and his team spoke with hundreds of student leaders and committees, and gained their commitment to both participate and encourage others. He got the initial commitment by sharing snackable content—just enough to get them interested and involved.

Joe said, "When you start a change, present it in a way that is very simple and easy to understand. You don't have much time to get their attention. Make it a simple thing to agree to." At this early point you are first requesting involvement—an ongoing commitment will come in time.

This cultural reality of speed is in direct conflict with the long-established habits of many groups operating today. Traditionally, changes are decided by someone in charge, then passed to the next level and the next level over the course of weeks or even months.

Charley Johnson, Wave Maker and president of the Pay it Forward Foundation, described how quickly conditions and the world are changing: "I really want the people who read your book to know that we are in a completely different time now—even in the last five years. Every month, something new is thrown at us. The more I'm out talking to people, the more I'm convinced that you literally have to be okay with one month thinking you're right, and then the next month looking in the mirror and realizing, 'I was so wrong'. And, then feeling confident going in a different direction."

When you plan your change, know that short attention spans require that you grab interest quickly. Get to the "why" and to how your audience can get involved in a compelling and simple way. Also, consider that the importance of visual stimulation is increasing. According to KISSmetrics, photos on Facebook get 39 percent more interaction than text-only posts.[10] And an analysis by M Booth reports that videos are shared twelve times more than links and text posts combined.[11] The ten-paragraph e-mail and the forty-page presentation will work against you as the expectation for short but interesting nuggets increases.

But don't let the shorter attention spans and need for speed affect your expectations for results. Change takes time. Be patient and persistent while understanding that you have a very distracted and busy audience on your hands.

Tory Johnson—Wave Maker, #1 *New York Times* best-selling author, *Good Morning America* weekly contributor, and successful entrepreneur—shared her view on the pace of our society and change: "I think too often we give up too quickly because change doesn't happen fast enough. Success doesn't come quickly enough. We're in this society where we want things fast. You want to get rich? Buy a Powerball ticket. That's your fastest way to become rich. You want to be a singing sensation? Go try out for *American Idol*. Everything is about the fastest way to achieve what we want. Real life doesn't happen that way. Real life takes a long time to make things happen." Find ways to incorporate fast and bite-sized, but don't assume your change will follow suit.

What does this trend toward brief content mean for you and your change? Here are some suggestions:

- Build early interest.
- Share your story in bite-sized pieces. Dribble out information that builds interest and commitment over time, rather than in one sitting. You can go into more detail later when needed, but start with the headlines and purpose to build interest and then phase in more detail.
- Make sure the "why" and the impact to the individual are clear.
- Know how your audience prefers to consume information and collaborate. Assume that the majority will appreciate short and sweet in this busy and distracted world.

Intense Personalization

The era of personalization and individual choice has been growing for some time: we design our own car features and phones, custom build athletic shoes, and create our own magazine of interests on Pinterest. And this trend continues in our media consumption habits. We watch the TV shows we want to watch when we want to watch them, select only the news of interest, and pick the apps that fit our needs. This growing trend drives a continued shift from "one size fits all" to "one size built to fit your select group." Or even you alone.

The balance of power is shifting. A realignment is underway between the consumer and corporate interests. Corporations and businesses are no longer in the driver's seat regarding what information is shared and what consumers can access. Now, we largely all have access to the same information anytime, anywhere. Consumers can shop and compare the entire market in real time on their mobile devices. This phenomenon is changing entire industries. Many electronics stores that were thriving ten years ago have turned into showrooms for Amazon or other online retailers. Some have closed their doors. Customers increasingly do competitive pricing online and, if they need to, check out the product in a local store before going home to order it.

We recently purchased a used car for our new sixteen-year-old driver, Patrick. We looked at an integrator site to sort all of the cars in our area for style, model, price, and other features that mattered to us. After we knew what we wanted, we went off to the car dealerships, a trip I dreaded. I had memories from past years of waiting while the salesperson went away to agree on a price with the finance manager behind the glass wall—but only if you buy today. We visited a few dealerships and I couldn't believe how different the experience was from those trips of the past. Every dealership now posts all cars online, so the prices are almost identical at each one, and the cloud of mystery has been lifted. It made for a much more pleasant buying experience because all customers have access to the same information, which isn't filtered through a car dealership. The consumer is in the driver's seat and expects to personalize the type of information that is valued. Personalization has entered a new era, one of hyper-personalization, which goes beyond the demographics of a market segment to individual preferences and identity. The goal is to communicate and engage with customers on what they are interested in and leave the other information behind. Disney recently captured headlines with its bold move into hyper-personalization with the debut of MyMagic+ at Walt Disney World in Orlando, Florida. According to JWT Intelligence, a trend research and analysis company:

> The new system includes a new website and app, My Disney Experience, designed to give visitors a quicker, less stressful experience at the park (e.g., letting people preselect FastPasses for shorter wait times and VIP seating). The feature that's capturing the most attention, and raising a few eyebrows, is the optional RFID (radio frequency identification) bracelet, or MagicBand, which can function as park ticket, FastPass, room key, and credit card if users opt in. Those who do so will enable Disney to create a highly personalized experience—for example, employees will be able to address guests by name, thanks to sensors that pick up MagicBand data. Robotic seagulls will even strike up conversations with MagicBand wearers in line for the new ride Under the Sea.[12]

I'm a big Disney fan, and the personalized experience sounds appealing because Disney World can be a fun but overwhelming experience—though I'll pass on the personalized chat with the robotic seagulls.

Regardless of our views on privacy—which is a growing concern as personalization spurs intensive data collection—this trend toward more and more personalization will continue to grow, driving up our expectation that our experience will be customized specifically to our individual interests and preferences.

Personalization will affect how you approach your wave. Those engaged in the wave with you—and those you want to engage—need to see that the change matters to them and involves the issues that they and their group care most about.

Here are some ideas for how this trend toward personalization might affect your change:

- There will be more individual conversations to discuss the personal impact and gather individual feedback.

- Small group discussions with those who have common interests will be critical.
- There is unlikely to be just one big story or presentation; instead, there will be more adaptations for smaller groups that reflect their interests.
- Acknowledgement of smaller groups, or even individuals, rather than a monolithic group will be key.

Our expectations for personalization and for products and services that fit our unique needs will only increase. Your change must acknowledge individual differences while staying focused on the core meaning of your wave.

Personal Endorsements and Word of Mouth

Research tells us that we listen to the recommendations of those we know much more than to advertising campaigns or packaged communications. As a result, companies hope that a friend's recommendation shared on social media will encourage you to check them out.

According to a study by Ernst & Young, "People trust their friends and family much more than they trust corporate marketing media. Peer recommendations—not paid-for advertising, whether on social media platforms or in print—are what count." The report emphasizes that, while personal recommendations have always mattered, their value is increasing. The study stated:

> Personal recommendations have, of course, always been important. But the internet means they are more potent than ever. The "social consumer" no longer shares their viewpoints with just a close circle. They share good or bad retail experiences online, where they are seen—and passed on—by countless friends of friends. Likewise, those with many followers on Twitter or their blogs can have an influence far beyond their own postings, if they are trusted by large numbers of followers who can, in turn, pass on their commentary and opinions to their own followers.[13]

Of course, this principle of social experience applies to us too, whether online or in person. If we hear a personal recommendation to join a discussion group, participate in a community event, or sign up for the employee action team, we are much more likely to respond. The recommendation becomes a personal invitation to get involved.

A few years ago, my friend Laurie Axford asked me why I wasn't part of a local women's community service group. I had considered it many times, but there was no impetus to take action. I was already very busy and not looking for ways to fill my time. But Laurie called me personally and encouraged me to get involved. She said she thought I could make a real contribution and she emphasized the group's impact in the community. Then, she said, "Would you like to come with me to a meeting next week and see what you think?" She came and picked me up. Guess what? I joined, though I would never have gone without her personal invitation.

In a recent Nielsen study on the advertising we trust the most, the highest-rated source, at 90 percent, was recommendations from those we know personally or who are in our social networks.[14] With those endorsements there is no agenda, just a personal recommendation to try the new restaurant, see a great movie, or read that newly released book. Personal recommendations are likewise needed for any change to build momentum and take hold.

Wave Maker Brett Hurt is co-founder of Bazaarvoice, a company based on encouraging word of mouth in retail through customer comments. Brett shared a story about an early sales call he had with a potential client who didn't buy into word of mouth: "In late 2005, I was on the phone with one of the oldest companies in the U.S. The customer says, 'Brett, do you think I'm going to allow people to say whatever they want about our products? We don't sell anyone else's products—it's just our brand!' I put the phone on mute and told our salesperson that this plane is going down. And then I have this eureka moment."

Brett asked the client if he had heard the story of Kryptonite bike locks. He hadn't, so Brett told him about this very successful brand of bike locks marketed as being indestructible. Yet one day just one customer posted a YouTube video showing how to easily break a Kryptonite lock using a Bic pen. According to Brett, "Kryptonite evidently didn't know about it. Weeks later the video went viral and became their number one search result on Google. Kryptonite learned about it and decided to address it with a multimillion dollar recall representing one third of their sales! I asked my client, 'Do you want to be Kryptonite locks? Or do you want to know as soon as there's a problem? Don't you want to know that? And don't you think people are already talking about you whether it's online or not?' There's a moment of silence on his end. And then literally a very tense minute passes. And he finally said, 'We'll do it.'"[15] Brett knew that this was a turning point for Bazaarvoice and its mission to "change the world, one authentic conversation at a time."

Following are some steps that will help you capitalize, in your wave, on the trend toward personal recommendations:

- Identify the key influencers and involve them early. Their agreement and interest will affect others.

- Identify a plan for positive word of mouth. We'll share some ideas on how to do this in chapter 7.
- Remember, when you consider momentum builders for your change, that one of them could be the involvement and engagement of the right people. We'll learn more about creating those momentum builders in chapter 6.

Human Connection

The more time we spend staring at our computer screens and phones, the more valuable and unique personal and human interaction becomes. In a recent conference Ann Mack, director of trendspotting for JWT Intelligence, said, "As we spend ever more time in the digital world, what's becoming increasingly valued is the time we do not spend in front of a screen—the time we spend with real people and real things. It's not that we're abandoning digital—far from it. But as we buy more apps, e-books, and downloads, and as digital screens become our default interface with the world, we seem to increasingly seek out physical objects and experiences."[16]

The access to media anytime and anywhere has lowered the number of in-person connections we have. How many times have you seen (or been) the family out for dinner staring down at their phones while waiting for their meal? Many of us spend the bulk of our days in front of computer screens. One-on-one, in-person interaction is being lost, and research shows we miss it.

According to Mack, people tend to utilize digital technology for its ease, speed, convenience, and cost. But the more we embrace the format, the more we miss the emotional qualities it has a hard time replicating.[17]

We send an e-mail rather than make a phone call or talk in person. Handwritten notes are a lost art. I led a client workshop recently, and we all shared our most memorable celebrations of success. No one mentioned the big raise or awards dinner. We all mentioned the personal notes from people we respected or the special acknowledgement given at a team gathering. It reminded me that these simple human connections must be valued and remembered.

Mark Benton, a Wave Maker who redefined careers in R&D at PepsiCo, shared the importance of human connection in his wave: "I think one of our biggest factors in building momentum was being close to those most impacted by the change. And that meant I had to physically get out of my office—get on an airplane, get in a car, and find time to meet in person." Mark added, "We're in such a fast-paced world and there is a tendency to communicate through a device. You can't underestimate the power of being there in person."

The human interaction can be simple or obvious, but often forgotten. When you have a long list of 'to dos' for today, taking time for increased interaction can be viewed as an extra. But, even though there is no immediate gratification of completing a work task, the positive effects in your relationships can be long lasting.

Cynthia Young, a Wave Maker who led a culture change at an energy company, said, "Presence is important. Every morning when I got there, I did what I called my walk around. I walked up and down the aisles and said good morning to everybody. And I noticed when people were out or showed interest when someone was having a baby, and we'd talk about those things. I formed relationships. And with relationships come trust."

As personal notes and in-person conversations become the exception rather than the rule, these almost nostalgic methods of communication are becoming more highly valued. Here are some options for incorporating the human connection into your change:

- Know when an in-person connection rather than a virtual one is essential. Key sponsors and those who aren't yet on board will need a personal touch.
- Consider using techniques counter to trend that will be noticed. Examples may include a personal note, in-person conversations, or a thank-you phone call.
- Look for any retro ideas that will engage and involve others, such as forgoing a formal presentation for a visual aid or a personalized handwritten note rather than e-mail. I recently was invited to a luncheon to hear Colleen Barrett, the former President of Southwest Airlines, speak. In a world of podiums and dazzling PowerPoint presentations, Barrett quietly sat down in her wing chair, smiled at the crowd and said, "I thought we'd just talk today. I'll start and then I'd like to hear what's on your mind." She had no notes but it was one of the most impressive—and retro—presentations I have ever seen. Find the way to make your change simple, real, and memorable.

TRENDS THAT AFFECT HOW WE WORK TOGETHER

Now, let's examine a few trends that will affect how groups work together. Social media and generational differences are making groups function differently. There is more openness, sharing, and the traditional hierarchies within groups are experiencing a sea change.

Fading Hierarchy

Earlier we reviewed the conventional wisdom that all change comes from the top down. This trend is changing because our culture is placing less and less importance on the traditional hierarchy.

Social media has had a dramatic effect on leveling the playing field by allowing anyone to have a voice and a following. Anyone can have direct interaction with a favorite author, blog about politics, or have real influence as a customer. This ease of personal involvement reinforces that we all have a voice and that we can share or access useful information ourselves. It doesn't need to be filtered through an "expert" or an official source.

As we discussed in the trends that affect what we want, we value personal recommendations, access to information, and personal tailoring. These trends bump right up against traditional hierarchy.

Top-down decision making and communication are alive and well in many organizations today. In business, many processes and organizational habits began twenty to thirty years ago when business was more predictable and more hierarchical, and moved at a slower pace. Today, successful businesses must move at an incredible speed to stay competitive. The hierarchy and the command-and-control environment have become harder to sustain, giving way to a business culture with more flexible and accessible leadership.

In a recent *Forbes* article, John Kotter, the ultimate thought leader on leading organizational change, said, "Most companies are built with a strict hierarchy in place. This allows for managers to thrive and companies to excel at what they know and do best. But for organizations that need to change and quickly pursue new strategies, leaders must thrive, and they can only do so in a more dynamic environment, where traditional reporting structures take a back seat to good ideas, and where all individuals, regardless of rank, have the opportunity to help move the company where it wants—and needs—to go."[18]

More and more organizations are delayering. They aren't abandoning hierarchy altogether, nor should they, but they are reducing layers so that top leaders are closer to the frontline and to customers. Julie Wulf, an associate professor at Harvard Business School, issued a report on trends in organizational hierarchy after extensive interviews with CEOs. She reported that "CEOs offered several explanations for broadening their spans of control, but three themes were particularly relevant: to get access to information and bring more voices to the table; to more effectively drive change through the top team in rapidly changing business environments; and to assess and develop executive talent."[19]

While in this report many CEOs flattened the structure to be closer to the business, we know that innovation requires both new ideas and individual account-ability for starting change. Also, those closest to the business and the customer will have the best ideas for how to improve. Leaders need those recommendations to realize their goals.

Jonathan Morris, Wave Maker and president of a Young Presidents' Organization (YPO) chapter, introduced open sharing in what had been a competitive environment. He described how he translated what he has learned: "We are giving all of the YPO chapters an opportunity to share with one another. Why not do that in our own companies where we're using much more of a traditional, top-down structure? I realized it's just as important in my own company as well."

Cascading communications is the most common way that information is shared in organizations today. Communication starts with top leaders and works its way down level by level. This is how organizational hierarchy often operates in business today, but it doesn't work. It's slow and creates knowledge gaps vulnerable to misinformation. It also reinforces the attitude that the most senior people have all the answers. Such hierarchical communication works against the wave.

Clearly, organizations need some hierarchy and structure in order to manage the business. But don't assume that the hierarchy defines how your wave will grow and build momentum. It takes more than just the most senior people to enable a change.

Lois Melbourne, Wave Maker and co-creator and former CEO of Aquire, dis-cussed the power of her social network, which operates without regard to hierarchy:

> I remember talking to a CEO of a much larger organization than ours at a conference. Our meeting time had run out, so he said, "Please walk with me, we'll keep talking." And as we walked, lots of people were waving at me and saying hello. And he said, "How do you know all these people?" I said, "Well, I've been in the industry a long time, but the last two people who walked by are bloggers. I comment on their blogs and they comment on mine." He said, "I never read blogs, why would you ever read a blog?" I answered that it is how I know what's going on in our industry and what real people think, not just what's filtered through paid publications. He responded skeptically, "Ohhhh, okay." And that was a strong illustration of how separated some decision makers are from the real users of the prod-uct and their community.

Hierarchy made an appearance, even though the setting wasn't inside an organization.

Throughout *Make Waves*, I emphasize that others must not feel like spectators to your change. You need them to be part of it, to believe in it and feel committed. Consider hierarchy when it's needed and work around it when it gets in the way.

Here are some ideas for how to consider fading hierarchy in planning your wave:

- Involve those interested in your change throughout the organization, regardless of their position.
- Don't depend on cascading communications for large organizational changes.
- Identify influencers throughout the organization and externally who can get behind your change.
- Use social media to build interest in your company or idea, including internal social media tools that enable sharing and collaboration.

Peer Power

Social media and new technology have enabled growing networks of like-minded people to learn from each other and solve problems. Groups can easily come together around concern for an issue, area of interest, or cause. The concept that we can do more together than we can each do alone isn't new. But technology has made it so easy and fast to connect groups, even when members don't know one another.

In a recent *Wall Street Journal* article, Steven Johnson, author of *Future Perfect: The Case for Progress in a Networked Age,* notes "the growing prominence of a group of new organizations: fluid, collaborative networks working outside both the marketplace and the state to improve the world in inventive ways. Inspired in many cases by the decentralization of the Internet, the movement uses the peer network as its organizing principle, with no single individual or group in charge."[20]

Consider the trend toward user-generated content, including photo sharing and Wikipedia editing. Everyone contributes and no one is officially in charge.

This same concept carries over into work, as teams are expected to solve problems together without relying on a typical hierarchy. More and more companies are experimenting with employees sharing their knowledge using collaboration tools and encouraging employees to create interest groups based on their work or even outside interests.

Companies like Kickstarter have commercialized this idea by enabling anyone to invest in a new business through crowd funding. New business concepts are shared online, with access open to all. There is no middleman or approval board. Investors are those who believe in a concept and want to support it financially, and they choose how much to contribute.

Other companies use crowdsourcing to get fresh ideas for services, products, or content by requesting contributions from potential customers, typically online.

Lego, for example, introduced Cuusoo, a crowdsourcing platform that allows anyone to submit design ideas and encourages other users to vote on the designs. Once an idea reaches one hundred thousand votes, it receives a formal review by Lego and, if chosen for production, the person who submitted it receives a royalty. Walmart holds a contest designed to solicit crowdsourced inventions and new products. Companies are using such platforms to gather new ideas while also increasing customer engagement.

Another segment that is growing exponentially is the sharing economy, a system that offers shared access to goods, services, data, and talent. Peer-to-peer businesses like eBay and CraigsList let anyone become a retailer; likewise, sharing sites let individuals create an ad hoc car service, offer bike rentals, or share an extra bedroom as and when it suits them. The sharing economy is suited for widely owned expensive items by people who do not make full use of them. This commercialization of sharing creates access without a need for ownership. There is even a site where you can share your bow ties.

Rachel Botsman, author of *What's Mine Is Yours,* says the consumer peer-to-peer rental market alone is worth $26 billion.[21] And more established companies such as car rental agency Avis are exploring new options for consumer sharing outside their traditional business model.

Bob Wright is the founder of the Dallas Social Venture Partners (DSVP), a group of business professionals who make an annual personal contribution and then collectively decide the community groups they will support. He and a few colleagues decided that Dallas needed a better way to connect to community needs and engage a new generation of leaders. Their collaboration resulted in bigBANG!, an annual one-day forum that brings together business leaders, educators, nonprofit leaders, entrepreneurs, decision makers, and innovators to learn from one another, tackle the social issues challenging North Texas, discover who is doing what and how it's working, and become part of the solution to social challenges. Bob said, "One of our biggest momentum builders had nothing to do with us but was all because of a bigger wave that was already rising—the social innovation wave. We were on the forefront of that movement and it helped us build interest very quickly."

The trend toward social has implications for your change, as it reinforces team contributions and collaboration for greater impact. In chapter 7, we'll look at how to build a community around your change using this key trend toward greater team and peer involvement.

Here are a few examples of how you might harness this trend to start your change:

- Utilize crowdsourcing to generate ideas. Pose questions via technology to let others share their ideas, and offer some benefit for doing so.

- Empower the small group, which enables more sharing and collaboration.
- Aim for shared ownership to build a broad commitment for your change.

Virtual Reality

Virtual working—where individuals work from home, while "on the road," or outside traditional, centralized offices—is far from new, but it's an approach that has become more pervasive and more global in recent years. The evolution of working and engaging virtually has made it an essential factor in any change. According to a study by Aon, a consulting group for human resources and other services, over 40 percent of organizations expect virtual working to increase.[22] Most people in business are used to working seamlessly with colleagues in other locations, and some have never even met in person.

Today, one in five Americans works from home. Whether these are self-employed entrepreneurs running a small business or telecommuters affiliated with large corporations, more than thirty million of us work from a home office at least once a week. And that number is expected to increase by 63 percent in the next five years, according to a study by the Telework Research Network.[23]

And working outside the traditional office is becoming easier every day, as new virtual collaboration tools are simplifying the way we work together, even with colleagues on the other side of the globe. Technology has made our office mobile; it's wherever we happen to be. Teams can collaborate from any location at any time of day.

Your wave must address the virtual dimension of your change and not place too much dependence on physical presence. I recently saw a client initiative that had one location actively involved and engaged, but the other locations were on the margins even though they made up almost half of the workforce. They placed too much importance on those closest to their corporate office and top leaders and created bystanders in the other locations. The decision to unintentionally place a higher priority on one location than all others eventually undermined their change.

Consider the importance of virtual working and connection in your wave. Most changes today depend upon virtual teams and collaboration, so it's essential to consider that element when you plan your wave. Here are some examples of how you may use virtual tools to your advantage:

- Look for simple tools that will help your group stay in touch and share information easily, such as low-cost/no-cost videoconferencing.
- Create virtual discussion groups using the latest internal social media tools that are low or no cost.

- Make time for personal calls or videoconferencing in addition to the group calls, to help make the relationship seem closer in spite of physical distance.
- Learn more about the strategies and techniques for virtual leadership.

Demographic Tsunami

For the first time in history, there are four generations in the workforce, and sometimes even five. Baby boomers are working longer but will create a significant knowledge void as they retire in record numbers. Generation X, those born between 1965 and 1976, started their careers during a period of social and economic turmoil, and most resemble the millennials in their use of technology. They embrace the new and see the benefits of engaging. Millennials, which Pew Research defines as those with birth dates between 1977 and 1992, will make up approximately 36 percent of the U.S. workforce in 2014 and almost half of the workforce by 2020. These relatively new members of the workforce will come to dominate it in just a few short years and their impact will be transformative.

> "Gen Y doesn't have a lot of the same barriers and stereotypes that the generations before have. They're going to write a lot of their own rules."
> —*Kathy Korman Frey*

As Jeannie Meister and Karie Willyerd state so convincingly in *Workforce 2020*, "Never in the history of the modern world have there been four generations—much less five—in the workplace that bring such vastly different sets of values, beliefs, and expectations. And, never has a generation entered the workplace using technologies so far ahead of those adopted by its employer."[24] In addition to generational shifts in the workforce, the balance of genders is changing. Women still face issues with regard to career advancement and an equal playing field, but in 2010 women surpassed men on the U.S. payrolls for the first time in history. Despite record numbers of women in the workforce, little progress has been made in twenty years on the number of women at executive levels.

Ethnic diversity is changing drastically as well. Not only is there a dramatic change in workforces becoming much more global in nature, the racial and ethnic mix of workers in the United States is transforming. Between 1980 and 2020, the percentage of Caucasian workers in the United States will have declined from 82 percent to 63 percent. During the same period, the non-Caucasian portion of the workforce is projected to double, going from 18 percent to 37 percent, with Latinos almost tripling their numbers, rising from 6 percent to 17 percent.[25] The makeup of our communities and organizations is undergoing a seismic shift.

Organizations and businesses must adapt to a more diverse customer base and audience while ensuring that their practices are inclusive to all. Much more sophistication and tailoring will be essential. And, our previous section on personalization is so important in this changing workforce, as individuals look to products and services to meet their unique needs.

So, what do these changing demographics mean for your wave? Beware of starting with the way things have always been done. Even if your approach was successful in the past, remember the changing mix of generations, ethnicity, and gender. Consider who was missing from the conversation in the past that should be included now. Ensure that you aren't overly reliant on just one part of the community, market, or organization.

Here are some practical ideas for using this change in demographics to support your wave.

- Include and consider all generations, including the millennials, as you approach your change. While millennials may have less experience, they may have a fresh perspective you haven't considered.
- Look for ways to make the world smaller by including active participation from individuals in multiple countries.
- Ensure you include and incorporate a diverse set of experiences and perspectives in your change.
- Look at the change through the eyes of someone in a very different circumstance than yours to broaden your perspective and identify unique needs you may otherwise miss.

I hope that these trends encourage you to lift up and see that new ideas may work in your favor; experiment with them and identify where you need to learn more. There are so many new ways to collaborate, learn, and stay close to people thousands of miles away. Don't miss them in your wave.

THINK TIME

1. What trends most resonated with you?
2. What trends do you know least about?
3. What trends may affect your change?
4. What trends need some of your time, attention, and exploration?
5. How can you adapt the insights from these trends and make use of them in your wave?

PART 3

What You Do

Start. Move.

- Explore
- Know your why
- Find idea partners
- Keep it simple
- Have a bias for action
- Share with everyone
- Make it easy to say yes
- Don't expect consensus

Plan a wave that lasts

- Think big. Plan short.
- Know where you are
- Be an incrementalist
- Move without a perfect solution
- Experiment with a deadline
- Get points on the board

Create a community

Change that matters:
- Build around an idea that people care about
- Less WIFM, more WIFU (what's in it for us)

Team that cares:
- Encourage accountability
- Promote collective ownership
- Collaborate with intent
- Demonstrate mutual respect
- Use the magic of the small group

Team that shares:
- When we care, we share
- Translate with stories
- Talk straight
- Meet others where they are
- Combine enthusiasm with substance

DO

CHAPTER 5

Starting Your Wave

We've now looked how to define your wave and how important our thoughts are in making it a reality. We've also explored how trends in what we want and how we work will affect our approach. And, we've tested conventional wisdom to ensure that old tapes aren't getting in the way. Now, I hope you are ready for the most important decision—to get started. This first decision to act may be the most significant decision you make.

I've avoided using the word "steps" whenever possible because it implies that change is orderly and sequential. "Steps" makes it sound like there is a formula. There isn't. Instead, a wave is more like a natural flow, with dependencies that overlap and happen concurrently. Think of it like following dance steps, where you improvise and show your own style, rather than process steps that are precise, orderly, and sequential. With that caveat, let's get started.

LISTEN AND EXPLORE

Clint Hurdle, Wave Maker and general manager of the Pittsburgh Pirates, described his first step when starting as a new manager with a club like this: "You ask a lot of questions and then you really listen. It's a new environment with new players, why wouldn't you listen? Do you have all of the answers? Is there nothing left to know? Listening is how you gather real information before you decide what to do."

Understand the situation from more than your own perspective. Listen for what is working today and what isn't. Understand even more about the unseen opportunity before you begin to shape your wave.

Before you get to ideas, consider the world around you:

- Trends and changes that will affect the future
- Unmet or unspoken needs
- Goals and direction of the business
- Insights from other industries or situations that may be relevant

Understand the organization and its mission before you develop the ideas that will form your wave.

Cynthia Young, a Wave Maker who changed the culture of her organization through a passion for servant leadership, said, "I accepted the fact that I could be wrong and just listened. This is how I really understood the people and the issues." This point is important because you need to have a full understanding that your wave is needed, important, meaningful, or creates an opportunity.

Wave Maker Brett Hurt, co-founder of Bazaarvoice, explained that he had to thank Neal Kocurek, an Austin community leader and president and CEO of St. David's Healthcare System, whom he sought for advice a few months before Kocurek tragically passed away. Brett listened for wisdom and insights on two options he was considering at the time. Brett said: "Over lunch, I told Neal about both of my ideas for my next business. He said, 'I don't know anything about either one of the industries. But I can tell you're more passionate about the open community idea [Bazaarvoice] and you have many relationships in that industry from your Coremetrics experience. You are probably underestimating how valuable all of that knowledge is. You'll soon realize how important all of those connections are to you.'"

Brett said that after that lunch with a person he respected but didn't know well, his answer became clear. The insights he gained were not on the market need as much as on how he could be most successful in filling it.

Listening won't always give you all the answers, especially if your idea is new. Steve Jobs said, "It's really hard to design products by focus groups. A lot of times, people don't know what they want until you show it to them."

Like Brett, listen for information and meaning that you can translate for your wave, rather than looking for precise answers. Your idea may be different than what is imaginable today.

KNOW YOUR WHY

Your wave needs a bigger purpose and meaning at its core if it is going to last. This is how you build interest, stay motivated, and, most importantly, do something that matters. Think about the difference between the entrepreneur who starts his business because he sees a market segment opening from the one who wants to help customers be healthier and live longer. Of course, market need and financial opportunity are essential for the viability of any business, but a bigger purpose will make your wave sustainable for your customers and for you.

On the surface, Wave Maker Tory Johnson's change has been empowering other women entrepreneurs and, more recently, encouraging a healthy lifestyle. Yet, her community has grown because of her mission to help women learn how to get what they want in their businesses and in their lives. Wave Maker Bob Wright's creation of the bigBANG! event in Dallas caught on not because it was a great event—though it was—but because it was built upon connecting a new generation of leaders to community needs.

Many business leaders today depend on financial outcomes as the rallying cry they share with others. Of course, financials are at the core of a successful business. But you will need to define the meaning and purpose behind the numbers before others will commit and contribute.

> **"You have to be really clear about what you want to do and why. You have to know your 'why.'"**
>
> —*Tory Johnson*

At work, meaning can show up in different ways. I recently spoke at a client's Human Resources meeting, and participants gave a great example of how returning to meaning fueled their change. The company needed to attract more quality nurses in a very competitive market. In examining their "why," they realized that they were using their internal job descriptions, built for job leveling and pay, to explain the role to external candidates. They decided to return to the core reason nurses are nurses—they want to save lives and improve the health of others. This was their purpose. This decision set in motion a series of changes in the way they describe and market opportunities for nurses in their organization. This return to values gave them the answer.

A change that creates a groundswell of interest and has a positive impact needs meaning—values that won't be out of vogue next year. For example, a financial analyst's purpose may be to help her clients become financially secure, a nonprofit leader's may be improving literacy in his city, and a business analyst's purpose may be creating a more satisfying customer experience. Think about your change and your purpose together. Your purpose may lead you to your wave.

Wave Maker Lindsay Pender improved infant care in the neonatal ICU by importing ideas from her previous employer, a large metropolitan hospital, to her new smaller hospital. Lindsay's very simple purpose was to help the babies: "I knew that not everyone would agree with my ideas or want to change, but that if I—and we—kept our attention on the babies we could find a way to make progress."

Joe Nussbaum, Wave Maker and creator of the Big Event at Texas A&M University, had a similar experience. Joe said, "One of Texas A&M's core values is selfless service. I have a feeling that the Big Event helped influence service becoming one of the university's stated core values."

The "why" is essential to starting your wave. Integrate it into everything you say and do so that others remember it—and so you do too.

FIND YOUR IDEA PARTNERS

Finding Idea Partners doesn't mean finding others who are just like you, who think like you or who know what you know. If you find others who *want what you want*—that is enough for now. Find people who, like you, want to create the best learning environment for disadvantaged children, want customers to be integrally involved in product creation, or are committed to accelerating the advancement of women. Start developing a partnership with those who have the same core passion and purpose because those people have a built-in interest in your change.

> **"Pick the people who want to run with you and run fast."**
> —*Kate Rogers*

Author and entrepreneur Seth Godin says the others who want what you want are your tribe. He defines a tribe as a group of people connected to one another, connected to a leader, and connected to an idea. You aren't trying to create a tribe yet—that will come in time—right now you are looking for two or three Idea Partners committed to:

- Helping you determine how to solve the problem or seize the opportunity
- Sharing ideas
- Being actively involved from the start
- Being there for you to provide support, partnership, and collaboration
- Helping you spread the word and build an engaged community around your idea

When you identify your Idea Partners, include those who know what you don't know. Talk with people who look at the world much differently than you, both to learn and to test your assumptions. As one of my clients recently said, "There is wisdom to be gained from the opinions of others. Have a diverse circle and let them bring their wisdom to you in their own way."

> **"You need a short posse that's there with you."**
> —*Clint Hurdle*

Your change will likely take multiple capabilities, so someone involved in one part of your wave may not be essential in another. If your wave depends upon new technology, you'll probably need an Idea Partner with technology knowledge and expertise. You don't need a detailed solution yet, but you'll need contributions from someone who understands the possibilities and gives ideas that will eventually work.

You must be able to trust your Idea Partners, though they need not be your best friends. You want the right mix of needed knowledge and passion for the issues that you care about most. One of the best leadership teams I was part of had a diverse mix of personalities and styles. We trusted one another, but we didn't go to lunch together and we weren't best friends. We did respect one another, and I knew we had the smarts and the commitment to take on the challenges in front of us. That was enough.

Bob Wright, a Wave Maker who started the bigBANG! to connect a new generation of leaders to the Dallas community, said, "People asked what to expect when they came to the bigBANG! We said that you should expect that this will be the one place where you will see the suits talking to the creatives, and people standing around in jeans and in bow ties. It was going to be an eclectic mix of people. We had no idea how it would play, but people (for reasons I still don't understand) just trusted us."

> "I don't think we knew exactly what we wanted to do at first, but we knew we wanted to do something significant."
>
> —*Bob Wright*

The right Idea Partners collectively have more knowledge and perspective than any one person has alone. Involvement of this special mix of key people right up front greatly increases your chances of success. Fiona Grant, who started a wave that led to Accenture offering domestic partner benefits in the U.S. and ultimately changing global policies, shared how they got started. She said that the energy behind their recommendations began with two unrelated events. A key competitor introduced domestic partner benefits and a few weeks later the new Accenture CEO said he believed in bold change for the organization. Fiona said, "I went to a senior leader at Accenture, and said I really want to make a go at domestic partner benefits. Can we retry? Because it had been tried in the past, but unsuccessfully. We got a core team of people and started meeting regularly to put together our business case. Our group included one key leader who is a very strategic thinker. He advised us on how to create the right business case and get the facts we'd need. You have to have a little core group. If you were by yourself, it would be spectacularly hard."

> "Find a partner or two to do this with. Starting a change can be very lonely."
>
> —*Bob Wright*

PEOPLE SUPPORT WHAT THEY HELP CREATE

We use the expression "on the back of a napkin" for ideas drafted informally, and this type of casual dialogue is essential for building your ideas for change. Informal give-and-take allows others to be part of creating the idea, which is very different from shopping your idea to others. In my interviews with Wave Makers, I heard over and over that their idea first started over a glass of wine or in the back of a cab as they scribbled on a notepad or while chatting with a colleague on a long flight.

Surprisingly, no one I interviewed said that the change began in a formal brainstorming meeting, at a leadership summit, or even during a team meeting. Yet in business, we rely heavily on these more formal structured events to build engagement.

This back-of-the-napkin mentality works because it's an informal discussion with just two or three interested people, and there is no predetermined outcome. You are creating something new with others rather than trying to convince someone your idea is right. And these discussions offer a safe place to share unfiltered and untested ideas. The Wave Makers I spoke with often used language like, "I have an idea I'd like to share to see what you think about it."

As Guwan Jones said, when she was talking about her new ideas on diversity at Baylor Healthcare System, "I always approached my discussions with 'Here's what I'm thinking.'" This was her way of letting others know she wanted to explore the topic and was open to other ideas. It's much easier to test and create your change when you aren't recommending yet—you are noodling and letting others be part of shaping your idea.

> **"You're in trouble when it starts to be all about 'your idea.'"**
> —*Bob Wright*

Dan Roam, author of *The Back of the Napkin: Solving Problems and Selling Ideas with Pictures,* describes the experience of informal creation like this: "The reaction that you get from an audience is like magic, because they are with you, seeing the idea being built as opposed to coming in with a set of charts already prepared."[1] Think how different it is when someone says, "Let me show you the answer" versus telling you, "I have some ideas and would love to hear what you think," then invites you to shape the ideas together.

Going into a discussion with no previously defined outcome lets two or three people build on one another's thoughts rather than working toward an answer already in mind. While writing this book, I have had countless back-of-the-napkin conversations, and each one gave me a fresh idea or a new way to think.

Exchange ideas with those who have valuable perspectives—especially if those perspectives are different from yours. This kind of sharing can have an amazing effect on your change, activating and engaging first believers because they helped create the idea.

> **"No one likes to see your stuff and be told it's better than theirs. Don't do that. Even if you think it's true."**
> —*Jonathan Morris*

KEEP IT SIMPLE

Simple, clear goals will not only help you keep your focus but make it much easier to involve others. In this world of short attention spans and volumes of information, simplicity is essential. But creating clarity is more challenging than including everything but the kitchen sink. Fight the urge to favor complexity over simplicity, even though complicated plans can make us feel like the expert and reinforce our own importance.

My mother had an important surgery several years ago and her surgeon clarified the simple goal for the procedure before we began. He discussed her situation with us in a way that allowed us to make sound decisions together. This surgeon obviously had a wealth of detailed knowledge about her medical condition light years beyond what he shared with us. Yet he kept the goals and outcomes clear and understandable so that we could make informed decisions. Even complex topics benefit from simplicity.

Many big organizations naturally gravitate toward complicated goals that could be interchangeable with those of competitors. If your company does this, don't follow suit. A great simple goal for your change might be:

- I want to set up a forum with our customers in order to co-create better products.
- I want to give hope to children who are diagnosed with diabetes by helping them meet other active kids thriving after their diagnosis.
- I want every recruit to leave with a positive impression of our company and recommend us in the future, even if they don't work here.
- I want my new business to make technology simple and integrated for small business owners.

A simple goal can make decisions easier, make planning more straightforward, and help leave behind the extras that aren't essential.

I like the simple framework that Alan Siegel and Irene Etzkorn use in their book *Simple: Conquering the Crisis of Complexity.* The authors believe that there are three elements of simplicity:

- **Empathize**: understand others' needs and expectations
- **Distill**: boil down and customize what's being offered to meet needs
- **Clarify**: make the offering easier to understand, use and provide a benefit[2]

You have to empathize to achieve simplicity. Distilling and clarifying seem more intuitive, but empathizing connects simplicity to real meaning. You can't realize simplicity if you don't empathize with your audience. The best task force survey or detailed process analysis isn't enough.

In the early days with your Idea Partners, start with:

- What does my audience need?
- What is their experience today?
- How can I help simplify it?

Emma Scheffler, who started Insulin Angels while a high school freshman, knew the fear that children and parents feel when they are diagnosed with diabetes because she had been there. Parents have fears and questions like, "Will my child be able to be active, play sports, and just be like the other kids?" Insulin Angels pairs high school students with kids who are just diagnosed with diabetes to show them it's possible to carry on with active, healthy lives. Emma's empathetic response was to use the fears she and her family experienced to create a charity that addressed other families' deepest needs. Emma's change led with empathy.

Empathy takes imagination, sensitivity, and a willingness to look under the surface. In business, these can unfortunately be grouped with the "soft stuff," so they may slip down your priority list. Yet empathy is essential for finding your simple message and creating the impact you ultimately want.

Wave Maker Trisha Murphy Rae, who started Christmas is for Children, explained a key principle when asking people to help. She said, "You have to honor and respect others' time. Keep your requests simple and specific. Make it easy for people to help within a short amount of time. If you keep it simple, it's much easier for people to decide to get involved."

Keep that underlying need of your audience in mind, and use empathy to ensure you have a simple, clear, and compelling goal that fits your audience.

> "A person who leads a change has to have empathy for who they're impacting. And, as I learned more about what they needed, it made my vision bigger."
>
> —*Mark Benton*

PREDISPOSED TO ACTION

Wave Makers are predisposed to action, even when they don't have all the answers. Beginning before you know exactly where you're going can run against the conventional wisdom about the habits of effective leaders. It's counterintuitive for those who love to have the answer or who like detailed planning. But moving quickly is essential for Wave Makers.

Many of us earned our reputations and progressed in business because we are problem solvers. If you were the one at age ten waving your hand wildly from the back of the classroom because you had the answer, this is for you. Yes, I know it's painful. And if you have perfectionist tendencies, please try to contain them now. Remember that starting a wave isn't the same as earning an A or tackling your to-do list. It's starting momentum toward your goal and engaging others to be part of it. It's not a command-and-control effort. As a result, starting conversations with others early is essential—even before you have all the answers.

Lois Melbourne, Wave Maker and co-creator and former CEO of Aquire, shared the tension that can exist between gathering the facts and taking action:

I want to learn and feel like I can make a very educated decision. I read everything. Ask tons of questions. Do the research. Don't wait for perfect data—or even all of the data. When people think, "I just need a little more information," that drives me nuts. But at the same time, I don't make uneducated decisions. I feel like gut instincts come from assimilating a lot of information and then making the decision that you need to— even if at that specific moment you don't have all of the data. You know enough about the environment to be able to make an educated guess. That is enough.

> "I had no fear of asking questions. Because I knew
> I didn't have all the answers."
> —*Guwan Jones*

There are two important reasons that early action will help you to begin your wave and get others involves before you have everything planned:

1. Months four and five of the plan will change by the time you get that far anyway and you'll be a lot smarter by then—plus others will have new ideas that make your plan better.

2. Your change will never happen if it is just your idea and everyone else is a bystander.

Wave Maker Brett Hurt, an entrepreneur and co-creator of Bazaarvoice, shared the importance of movement:

You've got to get going. Surround yourself with other people who are incredibly passionate about your cause, and move. If you have a dream, you have to get moving or it's never going to happen. Now, if I'm looking to invest in an entrepreneur, for example, I'm looking for motion—someone who is really going after their dream and is passionate about it. They can approach it differently than me or have a different personality than me, but they have to be going after it. Let's get going. If you really believe in it, why not? Why aren't you moving?

> "Motion creates motion. Momentum creates momentum."
> —*Brett Hurt*

Also, you can't do this alone. Inviting others to be part of your wave—especially at the beginning—is essential. They'll make you smarter, and this is how the wave becomes "our" wave not just "your" wave. Become comfortable moving forward even without all of the answers.

If your wave is tied to big values, has meaning and purpose, and has a simple goal, you can and should start moving and sharing it with others. Almost all the Wave Makers I interviewed began sharing their ideas before they had all the answers. It was how they built a core team of Idea Partners and eventually a community that cared.

Wave Maker Bob Wright, founder of the Dallas Social Venture Partners (DSVP) and creator of the bigBANG!, started the idea but quickly let others be part of developing it. Bob and a few partners determined that they wanted the event to be like no other—no conference with static agenda, no talking heads, and no formal event. It had to be something that new generations in the community wanted to be part of, with the hope of their continued commitment.

Bob described how they got started: "We lived by the belief that we can't own and control this. We have to turn loose of the steering wheel and let others be part of shaping it. We crowdsourced the creation of this experience because we wanted a broader circle to feel responsibility for it."

Bob created a few informal events to start the discussion. He and his partners invited about twenty-five select social innovators to a discussion and asked for their participation. The invitation told them to invite anyone else who they felt should be included. Seventy-five people showed up for their first get-together. That meeting resulted in four Spark Clubs, idea-generating groups, which all contributed and helped develop the bigBANG!, shaping how it would work and its goal for community impact.

Bob and his partners at DSVP created a wave that people wanted to be part of and were involved in creating. The intent was defined and they knew their goals, but they let others create the how and the what. This example is so illuminating because they realized that it wasn't just about the event, it was about building the commitment to the cause. They let others help create and run it, and achieved more than even they had imagined in the beginning.

> "I could only see about the first 50 percent in the beginning. I couldn't have imagined everything we ended up doing. We took it step by step."
> —*Jonathan Morris*

SHARE WITH EVERYONE

Many Wave Makers described talking with "hundreds of people" about their idea. They viewed themselves as the personal advocate and interest builder for the project. No one mentioned the wonderful e-mail campaign or the jaw-dropping PowerPoint presentation; it all came back to personal conversations with people they trusted and who trusted them.

Share your ideas. Ask for other people's thoughts. Share with everyone what you are up to. As an example, if you are changing the hiring process at your company, start early by telling everyone the benefit of a transformed recruiting experience that creates future customers, rather than just weeding out candidates. Decide who can react to your ideas and help you learn more.

Allen Stephenson, a Wave Maker who founded Southern Tide while he was still a college student, shared his first actions and where he chose to spend his energies: "I stopped my social life, but I kept using my same social skills. I just started using them in a different way. I met anyone I could who might know someone or wanted to help in any way. I'd ask them for advice or ideas and I helped them any way I could too. "

Allen continued, "I talked to people who used to own apparel manufacturing companies, financial people, and so many others. I was taking people out to lunch like crazy—every day like three, four, or five people. And, some of them are still involved today. Obviously, I didn't find all of them myself, but that's how I did it. I didn't and don't know how to do all this stuff, but I did know how to say, 'This is the vision, the dream. We're going to do this and have clothes in the way that I'm describing and we can do this together.' "

When I started my business, I had a similar mind-set because I had so much to learn. I met with dozens of people individually and told them my plans. I asked for their advice and words of wisdom. Gibbs Mood, a successful business leader and a mentor from my time at Accenture, told me, "Don't get too clever and overthink it. Just tell everyone you meet what you are doing and your goals for your business. You never know what ideas you'll hear or where those conversations will lead. It's the hands down best way to get others interested in your plans."

He was right, though his advice was counter to much of the conventional marketing wisdom I heard at the time.

> "Never assume that once is enough. Repeat it over and over again until you think you have said it to everyone a million times."
> —*Joe Nussbaum*

Lois Melbourne, co-creator and former CEO of Aquire, accelerated her company's growth by engaging in social media to build relationships and a community within the HR software industry. She joined discussion groups, contributed to countless blogs, and met everyone she could.

Lois described her strategy:

Starting as an entrepreneur in a small company, I did every trade show. And where a lot of companies didn't find trade shows a very good return on investment, they were the best investment we made. It was because we used them differently. We used them to meet everyone. I would go and meet people, not just customers, but I would get to know everyone in every other booth. I'd learn what they do, why they made certain decisions, and who their buyers were. And by getting to know people, and by being open, I built a network of people who referred customers or great employees to us. And the sales reps on a trade show floor become sales managers, CEOs, and executives. And by then, they were our friends. My network grew up with me as they also moved up the ranks and moved around in different companies.

Lois followed this principle: meet everyone. Tell everyone. Listen. Her approach created a network and community of people interested in Aquire's business.

Talking to everyone and engaging the right people, in person or through social media, helps create early interest, but can also make your ideas more real. Joe Nussbaum, who created The Big Event at Texas A&M University in 1982, described his approach to these conversations: "I told so many people about it that the idea became legitimate in a very short amount of time."

MAKE IT EASY TO SAY YES

Allen Stephenson started Southern Tide as a twenty-two-year-old college student after spending a semester abroad in Italy. In Florence he saw fashion that was dramatically different in look and quality from what he knew at home. When he returned to South Carolina, the American fashion he had worn growing up looked new and vibrant. Even though he was a biology major with plans to go to medical school, Allen regularly took his polo shirts apart and reconstructed them so they would fit just right. He began to connect the quality and construction of clothing he had seen in Italy to the American style he had always known. His desire was for a better polo shirt—one that looked better, fit better, and felt better.

When Allen first began, he created prototypes and went to M. Dumas & Sons, a premier clothing store in Charleston, South Carolina, carrying his prototype shirts in a Gap bag—nothing was even branded yet.

Allen said:

> I asked to talk to the store manager and said, "I have these shirts I'd like to show you." He told me that the last thing he needed was another polo shirt. I said, "I know—you're right. I'm not trying to sell you polo shirts." He was confused and wasn't clear where I was going. I said, "I'm going to give you these. I made them and I'm really impressed with them and I want to see if you are too—or if your customers are. Here's a dozen shirts in different colors and sizes. Just take them. Here's my number. Just give me a call if you get a chance and let me know what you think."

After a few weeks, Allen got a phone call from the manager at M. Dumas & Sons. The manager said that not only did they want to order some shirts, they were interested in creating a small wall to feature them. Allen said, "And, that was it. That was when I knew it was happening."

Allen's wave started because he didn't go for the hard sell. He made it easy to say yes. He gave a few shirts away at first so that the employees and customers at M. Dumas could try them. He let the product speak for itself.

> **"We moderated ourselves. We didn't ask for the world."**
> —*Fiona Grant*

When Bob Wright started the bigBANG! event for the Dallas Social Ventures Partners (DSVP), they began by inviting a few people to meet and talk about their plans. They didn't ask them to commit to be in a group, to join DSVP, or to sign up for a yearlong community service committee. They asked, "Will you come and talk about our idea?" That was it. And it was enough.

> "Communicate with clarity and conviction. Share what's in it for them. Confused people walk away."
>
> —*Tory Johnson*

DON'T EXPECT CONSENSUS

Of course, no group of people will agree on everything. When you set out to build your wave, this is important to remember. Assume you will face disinterest, resistance, and naysayers. We've discussed how to identify resistance, and some may interpret lack of agreement as resistance. It's not the same.

> "You have to manage the energy vampires and expect the naysayers."
>
> —*Julie Porter*

When it comes to change, consensus isn't the goal. Know where you need support, where you'd like it, and where it doesn't matter so much. I recently had a colleague tell me with disappointment that her ideas were shot down. After some questions, I learned that she had one meeting where she'd fielded some tough questions. She received some interest, but not across the board. She decided that it probably wasn't the right time based on that one discussion. Her expectations were probably unrealistic. Most new ideas will face skepticism. It isn't a reason to give up so soon.

Clint Hurdle, manager of the Pittsburgh Pirates, said the word "conflict" has a negative connotation, even though it's very important:

> Confrontation is really important in honest communication. As an example, if a base runner makes what looks like a poor decision, you have to confront it—but do it in the right way. The first thing I do is ask the question, "Tell me what you saw out there," and I listen to the answer. Then, the next day we look at the tapes together and match that up to what he saw at the time. This is a chance to learn. And it's a lot more effective than yelling at a player, "That was a stupid play" in front of the team as he comes into the dugout. He knows he made a mistake. Confrontation in the right way is how we learn and understand each other.

Rather than use a lack of consensus as a setback, learn from it and decide if you can move on without it. Mark Benton, a Wave Maker who redefined careers in

R&D at PepsiCo, explains how he balances listening and respect with persistence: "You have to have a deep respect for people. We all want to be heard. If I give others the respect and the dignity of hearing them out, then I feel like they need to give the same to me. Then, hopefully, we can all come to an agreement that will accomplish something, but you won't get everything. And, ideally, we'll find some common area to agree or compromise."

Mark summarized, "We don't have to agree, we just need to understand each other. If we understand each other, there's potential for us to get something done."

Most Wave Makers have no expectation of full consensus, but understand that many waves need sponsorship to make progress. In studying Wave Makers, I found that they use strategies to keep them moving forward even without consensus. They:

- Use individual collaborative conversations more than group "selling"
- Listen to understand another point of view, even if they don't agree
- Ask for early input of key people so it is considered and included up front
- Accept that some people won't be on board, treat them respectfully, and find a path to move forward (in my interviews, I found that many of the initial naysayers became supporters after there was some success; the initial lack of support can change over time)
- Take small but deliberate steps rather than going for that one big formal decision that could shut the effort down before it was fully understood

Every organization is different. But, in any situation, you have to keep the naysayers in perspective.

Tory Johnson, Wave Maker, entrepreneur, author, and *Good Morning America* weekly contributor, said:

I think politicians recognize this. They're never going to get 100 percent of the vote, or even 60 percent. People in sales know they're never going to make 100 percent of the sales. Ballplayers know they're not going to score on 100 percent of their attempts. That's all okay. You just have to be able to score enough points to win. Get enough people on your side for victory—enough people to believe in your cause to bring about the change. When you never solicit feedback, you don't have the opportunity to understand who's on your team. You can't just bulldoze your way to making good things happen.

Keep the need for approval or agreement in perspective. Paul Zellner, a senior executive at Russell Reynolds, has been a friend and advisor of mine over the years.

I asked him to speak to my company about growing relationships and clients, as Paul is an expert in this area. One of his points really stuck with me. He talked about the importance of embracing "Oh well." He said that he has learned that you can't take a lack of interest personally or assume that you'll never make progress. He reminded us that everyone has individual priorities and an agenda, which may not fit yours. Of course, learn from every interaction, but sometimes you just say, "Oh well. I tried to build a relationship" or "I tried to introduce a new idea and it didn't work that time." It doesn't mean it never will or that you made a mistake. Learn from it and carry on. You don't need everyone's approval to reach your goal.

> **"Any change will have nonbelievers at first, or it would have been done already."**
>
> —*Jonathan Morris*

THINK TIME

1. What opportunity do you see that no one is asking for today?
2. What values are undeniable in your organization or community?
3. What values do individuals in your organization or community believe in?
4. Who cares about the same issues that you care about?
5. What gaps in knowledge do you have that can be addressed by others?
6. Who are three to five people who are natural Idea Partners for your wave?
7. What opportunities do you have or can you create for informal conversations with your Idea Partners to develop ideas or options?
8. What simple goals can you share with others?
9. How can you prepare for involving others without developing the answer in isolation?
10. What resistance can you expect and how can you plan for it?

CHAPTER 6

Planning a Wave that Lasts

You've started. You are past the hardest part—deciding to act. You've addressed your fear of taking action, developed an idea that matters to you and others, and found your Idea Partners. Now it's time to build on your momentum and start a change that will last.

You're ready to experiment, plan, and build sustainable interest. Most planned changes never make the leap from great idea to reality. Some research says only three out of seven change initiatives succeed; the classic statistic is that 70 percent of initiatives fail. We can debate the exact number, but what's clear is that many intended changes never come to fruition. In this chapter, we'll look at how to plan and organize your wave so that it lasts.

> **"Ideas are a dime a dozen. It's all about execution."**
> —*Tory Johnson*

Make Waves presumes that anyone can start a change—it can start at the top, but that's not the only place. Of course, some changes need sponsorship and a broader coalition to gain traction. Be sure that your wave has "legs" so that it will be implemented and become a reality. Much like the human wave at a ballpark or a rock thrown into a pond, the ripples of a change continue well beyond the starting point. How far can you take it?

In many new businesses, the entrepreneur who created the concept or idea eventually must bring in someone else to run the business. It takes a very different set of skills to lead and operate a multimillion dollar business than to envision, create, and sell the concept to the market. You know the story of Mark Zuckerberg and Facebook. Once Facebook became a real company with plans to go public, he needed Sheryl Sandberg to be COO. He didn't step away from the business, but he had a great partner to manage the business with him. This partnership is relevant even on a smaller scale. It's important right up front to consider what you can do and where you'll need expertise and involvement from others.

I've included Think Time questions for each section in this chapter to help you reflect on your plan specifically as we go through this topic together.

THINK BIG, PLAN SHORT

Before you start developing your plan, envision the impact. Describe what is happening when you reach your goal. If you know your desired future, then start making short- term decisions that will move you forward in the right direction. And, make the necessary ongoing adjustments to get you there. You may also learn that even your vision may change and increase as you learn more and make progress.

Here are key questions to ask yourself before you develop the next phase of your plan:

- What is my vision and desired impact? How will I know when it is realized?
  - Financial
  - Service
  - Process or effectiveness
  - Engagement
  - Other relevant metrics (quantitative and qualitative)
- How has your vision changed or updated based on valuable input from others?
- What can I do? What is in my control?
  - Where do I need others?
    - Support
    - Sponsorship
    - Resources
    - Knowledge
  - Who isn't involved but should be?
  - If anything stops my wave, what will it be?

These few basic questions can help you focus as you organize and plan for progress.

Let's plan your wave. As we discussed in the previous chapter, planning too much detail far in advance can actually work against you. Most waves are unpredictable and hold surprises. Stay flexible and be prepared to adjust. Of course, large-scale changes need key milestones and rigorous planning, but don't let your desire to plan too far out affect your adaptability.

Plans are created with a certain set of assumptions that will change over time. We can become very attached to a plan once it's agreed and in place. I was in a discussion recently when the team realized that their original plan was based on old assumptions that had never been updated. Since the plan was originally created, conditions had evolved and the company had new faces with new expectations. The environment had changed, but the team and their plan hadn't.

Also, we know the importance of inviting others to be part of your wave. A wave is not a command-and-control effort. Others must believe that they have a vital role to play.

> **"The worst thing you can do is show up and say, 'Good news, I have all of the answers.'"**
>
> —*Jonathan Morris*

YOU ARE HERE

At large shopping centers there is a dot on the map that says, "You are here." It tells me where I am and shows me the path to J.Crew. Of course, my starting point will determine my route and how long it will take me. You need to know the same about your wave from two perspectives: How big is the change for you? And how big is the change for your organization or community?

Let's start with your personal starting point. How big is this wave for you? How big is the gap between where you are today and where you want to be?

A former colleague left her career as a chemical engineer and became a teacher so she could help students develop an interest in math and sciences in the early high school years. She knew the topic really well, but moving out of business and into education was a huge change for her. She had to learn how to instruct students, collaborate with other teachers, and understand a completely different audience, including parents. For her, the gap to a new working environment was big. She learned to continue to rely on her expertise, but developed a completely new approach for how she shared it.

A friend of mine started a complete health overhaul for herself and her family. She began by setting a goal to run a 10K race in one year. She had a big gap from her starting point because she was fairly inactive, but she gave herself enough time to prepare for the race. She knew that with commitment and work she could do it. It was a high hurdle and a challenge that stretched her out of her comfort zone.

> **"Just like a workout routine, the hardest part is getting started."**
>
> —*Melisa Miller*

Emma Scheffler, the Wave Maker who started Insulin Angels as a high school student, knew nothing about starting a nonprofit, but she had an idea and a passion. She had to rely on others to help her set up the organization and make it a reality. Her parents, Lisa and Leon Scheffler, were there to help and guide her. But, the gap didn't keep her from deciding to act.

Also, consider the starting point of your organization or community. How big is the change for everyone involved? How will that affect your approach and timing? The gap between where you are today and where you want to be will affect your plan.

Fiona Grant knew she was taking on a big change when she and her team set out to convince Accenture senior leadership to introduce domestic partner benefits. Fiona saw the broader commitment to diversity and a CEO who spoke of bold change, yet it was a relatively conservative Fortune 500 management consulting, technology and outsourcing firm. She worked closely with others who cared about this issue. They developed a thorough business case based on facts and extensive research. She knew that, given the magnitude of the change, it would take a comprehensive and well-thought-out recommendation with facts to back it up. She knew her starting point and developed her plan accordingly.

THINK TIME

1. What is your starting point? Where are you today?
2. How dramatic is the change you want to pursue?
3. Does your group or organization feel the need for your change yet or do you have to create the need?
4. How equipped are you to pursue this change?
5. What knowledge, information, or partnerships do you need based on where you are today?
6. How will your starting point affect your timing?

BE AN INCREMENTALIST

A change takes a plan, but it's not your typical project plan. Keep your destination in clear focus as you develop your plan—much like the route on a map. You plot and adjust your route as you know more about conditions and needs. Think about an offensive coordinator in football who has his team prepared based on a game plan to exploit the other team's defensive coverage. But on game day the team realizes that their opponent has made major adjustments and has changed their typical defensive schemes. The coach will have to make game-time adjustments and experiment in real time to see what works.

> "The plane was moving and we were absolutely building it while we were in flight."
>
> —*Mark Benton*

The best plans for a wave are incremental—reacting to new and changing conditions—yet aimed toward the big goal. Incremental planning is:

- Future focused
- Adaptive and flexible
- Short horizon, with long-term goals in mind
- Collaborative

Kate Rogers, the Wave Maker who started the wave of health and wellness at H-E-B Grocery Stores, said that they knew they were taking on a big change by asking employees, leaders, customers, merchants, and partners to make H-E-B their health and wellness destination. Kate said, "We prioritized, and everything we did was incremental. We knew that it took time to bring people along. It was the most iterative process ever."

Incremental planning assumes you make those adjustments as you go and still reach your goals—even if they change over time. Some Wave Makers started their wave and not only made notable changes along the way, but changed their destination because the potential was much greater than they'd ever imagined.

> "We were incrementalists. We knew our goal and we got there step by step."
>
> —*Fiona Grant*

Melisa Miller, Wave Maker and EVP and president of Alliance Data Retail Services, took on a major change by committing her team to doubling the division's business in five years. They knew it would take a clear plan, but they also wanted to change the culture. At the beginning, it was very clear that the business outcomes were a given. Melisa told her team, "We will discuss how we get there, but not the destination."

Here are some tips for finding the right balance between no plan and too much structure:

- **Have very clear outcomes**, even if you decide to adjust them over time. Keep your goals simple and know where you are headed.
- **Balance specific plans with flexibility** so that your decisions are actionable, but keep in mind that changes will likely be made. A change to the

plan isn't a mistake, it's to be expected. You aren't necessarily changing your destination, just how you get there.

- **Take frequent looks at the future.** Adjust the plan frequently as those in the wave share progress with one another. The most important conversation starts with: "Based on what we have learned and where we are going, what adjustments are needed?"
- **Begin without all the answers,** as we discussed in the previous chapter. It's essential to start before you have it all figured out, and almost all Wave Makers I spoke with did so. This can help you get a better answer and build your coalition before you are well into execution.
- **Remember the human side of planning,** not just the deliverables and actions. Wave Maker Eric Buhrfeind said he talked to hundreds of people individually and in groups about his idea. While the conversations were informal, he also tracked the people he had spoken with and those he still needed to contact. Guwan Jones preferred individual conversations with important contributors because she felt they were essential in learning what needed to change, not just to sell her ideas.
- **Keep a Goldilocks mind-set**—not too hot, not too cold. Your goal is a flexible, thoughtful, and organized path to change that involves others who feel part of the wave. Avoid flying by the seat of your pants on one extreme and an overengineered, inflexible plan on the other. Find the happy medium and feel comfortable there regardless of your own personal preferences.

> **"I always reserve the right to get smarter."**
> —*Mark Benton*

THINK TIME

1. Do you have a clear outcome? How can you describe it?
2. Who needs to be involved in your planning?
3. What is your go-to planning style and does it fit an incrementalist approach?
4. What adjustments do you need to make in your personal style for a wave?

MOVE WITHOUT A PERFECT SOLUTION

In chapter 2, "Think Like a Wave Maker," we talked about perfectionist paralysis—the mind-set that says, "until it's perfect, I can't begin." Decide when 80 percent is good enough to get started. There are some situations when you need to be 100 percent certain of your course, such as when you are making financial recommendations to your client, or when the issue concerns legal matters, quality, or character. But what about the rest? Wave Makers move before they feel completely ready because of a bias for action and progress.

> **"I've found that my gut instinct is a lot more reliable when I've assimilated lots of information."**
>
> —*Lois Melbourne*

Lori Meyers, a Wave Maker who heads up Chase's Place School, became president of this unique school for children with developmental disabilities. She explained that, at first, she just didn't know enough to do everything at 100 percent. Her comment has stuck with me: "I finally decided that my 60 percent could make all the difference, and it was enough. I just kept going." Your 60 percent may be enough to make notable progress, not because you don't want to give 100 percent, but because 60 percent is all you know how to do or that time allows.

Also, some waves are part of much bigger changes, so the assumptions are constantly changing. If you wait for the perfect solution, the parameters will have changed by the time you can begin implementing it.

An adaptable and flexible planning approach allows you to adjust your plan over time and aim for your 80 percent—and maybe eventually your 100 percent. When I was a new entrepreneur, I learned so much so fast that I was giving 150 percent, but my contribution was about 60 percent because I didn't know what I didn't know. By staying flexible, I compensated and adjusted as I learned more rather than sticking with my original plan or my original definition of success.

> **"Our plan evolved and it was a little bit like a chess game. What piece do we move next? Why are they voting no on this and what can we do about it?"**
>
> —*Kate Rogers*

Bob Wright, Wave Maker and creator of the bigBANG! community event in Dallas, said, "We tried to be inclusive from the outset. We never tried to openly own the idea. We went into meetings with our partners and co-conspirators with about 80 percent of what we wanted. We allowed them to mold the other 20 percent, and I think they felt like they owned 50 percent. It became community owned before it became community questioned."

Lori Myers, of Chase's Place School, shared a favorite quote from Tina Fey's book *Bossypants*. Lori said Lorne Michaels's advice resonated with her: "The show doesn't go on because it's ready; it goes on because it's 11:30."[1] There are times when the opportunity or the deadline arrives whether we are ready or not. You have to move quickly to reach your goals.

Think about it: If you had to make one move, what would it be? Decide how you can begin to make some progress now. The first step is the hardest.

Wave Maker Lindsay Pender spent six years as a neonatal ICU nurse at one of the top metropolitan hospitals in Philadelphia before moving to a smaller town and much smaller hospital. She believed that what she had learned previously would be valuable to this smaller hospital, which didn't have access to the resources and technology of the much larger hospital.

Her first step was to ask other nurses and respiratory therapists if they felt specific practices in the neonatal ICU nursery were working. She also talked to a more senior leader about ideas that she felt would help the babies in ICU, and she received a receptive response. She then joined a task force that focused on improving processes and procedures. She was thoughtful about her first steps, so she made progress while recognizing that she couldn't make these changes alone. She knew that she wanted to start a change, but she didn't want to be the "know it all or put anyone down." Lindsay didn't look for the perfect solution, she found a way to get started and make progress.

> "I knew I wanted to start a change. I just found what I thought was the best way to get started."
> —*Lindsay Pender*

THINK TIME

1. If you had to take one step to get started, what would it be?
2. Who may be helpful to you in taking those first one or two steps?

EXPERIMENT WITH A DEADLINE

Because waves are new, they require experimentation and probably some failures. Remember that a wave is different from a project or initiative. A wave is about changing your community, organization, business, or the lives of others for the better. As a result, it isn't sequential and orderly. It will take some experimentation and testing to see what works and what doesn't—but you need a deadline.

An experiment is a test, trial, or tentative procedure for the purpose of discovering something unknown or of testing a principle or supposition. Experimentation must be timely and quickly serve as input for your longer-term plan. It isn't a reason to lose ground or delay as you continue testing and looking for the perfect answer. Unless you are in a research role that requires a predefined time frame for testing, use testing to confirm that your change is sound, try your boldest ideas, get others involved in the experiment, and learn before you share more broadly. But remember that timeliness and speed are usually an essential element in momentum. Your experiment must consider timing and the feedback needed before you begin.

The purpose of an experiment is to test your hypothesis and determine whether your assumptions are correct. While you may not follow each step in the scientific method, your trial must have a clear purpose and identify the questions you expect to answer. This upfront time in planning will help you draw conclusions at the end.

Sim Sitkin, of Duke University, uses the term "intelligent failures" to describe experimentation and how we learn from trying and testing. Sitkin's criteria for intelligent failures are:

- They are carefully planned, so that when things go wrong you know why.
- They are genuinely uncertain, so the outcome cannot be known ahead of time.
- They are modest in scale, so that a catastrophe does not result.
- They are managed quickly, so that not too much time elapses between outcome and interpretation.
- Something about what is learned is familiar enough to inform other parts of the business.[2]

These criteria are meant for learning, quick interpretation, and action. Notice the key words "test," "trial," and "tentative." An experiment is not the same as an early release or pilot. The purpose is to learn and adjust.

> "When you experiment and lead a fundamental change, there will be lots of mistakes. Learn from it and keep going."
> —*Melisa Miller*

Waves require testing and experimentation because the ideas are new and often haven't been done before. Almost every Wave Maker I spoke with used experimentation and found it to be a fundamental ingredient in creating momentum.

Your experiment may involve sharing product ideas with potential customers, asking one hospital to test a new process for patient admissions, or trying a new recruiting experience in one division. Decide what you need your experiment to do—the questions to answer and the assumptions to test.

Experiments in one environment can be viewed as mistakes in another.

Melisa Miller, Wave Maker and EVP and president of Alliance Data Retail Services, emphasized, "We told everyone that we are going to make a load of mistakes because we are trying too many new things not to." Her team took on a multiyear change to reward risk and experimentation, which represented an important culture change. They made experimentation safe by communicating that it is valued and that mistakes are expected. Mistakes through experimentation are learning mistakes.

Experiments can also evolve into a pilot. One of the ways to create momentum and useful positive peer pressure is through a well-timed pilot. If one division tries a fresh approach for attracting new college recruits that receives interest and accolades—guess what happens next? Other divisions and groups start asking when they will be involved. Or, if one person in your business tries an interesting new way to involve customers and it works, then others want to know how they can do it too.

Be bold in your experimentation: step out a little. It's an experiment, after all, and you'll have time to adjust. This is the time to try your boldest ideas—you have the option to pull back before you activate more broadly, if you need to.

> "We experimented a lot. That is how we learned what would work, and we also learned that even great ideas sometimes don't."
>
> —*Kate Rogers*

THINK TIME

- What is your natural planning style? ("I want to know every step before I start" or "Who needs a plan?")
- How does your natural style fit with the need for specific but flexible planning for your wave?
- What adjustments will you need to make to ensure your approach is successful?
- Who else needs to be involved in planning your wave?

GET POINTS ON THE BOARD

Remember, the definition of a wave is a transfer of energy that creates momentum. A critical way of starting momentum is through visible early successes. In sports, teams like to score first to create an inevitability mind-set in their opponent and to build team confidence. The same is true in your wave.

In business, "quick wins" is one of the eight steps in John Kotter's classic business book, *Leading Change*. This element is important whether you are leading a big change from the top of the organization, creating a new business, or starting a wave in your community. Momentum builders are your wave's first impressions. Almost all of the Wave Makers I researched relied on momentum builders or some variation of quick wins for their waves.

> **"Get some early successes. It definitely buys you some time."**
> *—Jonathan Morris*

When Wave Maker Kate Rogers took on a wave, at the request of the company president, to make H-E-B Grocery the health and wellness destination for employees, partners, customers, and suppliers, she said, "We absolutely had to get some points on the board. We had created task forces and initiatives in the past, but we weren't making the progress we wanted. It was time to get moving. You can analyze things to death when you could be delivering something great."

Fiona Grant, a Wave Maker who led the creation of domestic partner benefits at Accenture, had a surprising momentum builder. It was a baby shower. Fiona shared the personal side of her story: "The big thing was that Heidi, my partner, became pregnant with our baby-to-be, Daisy. And she's a schoolteacher. But she decided that she was going to stay home. So I had a situation looming that was basically a personal need for me. I had to be sure they could both be on my insurance. I had to adopt Daisy, and that was complicated in itself. But I couldn't insure both of them for health insurance because there was no policy in place for domestic partner benefits."

She explained that a baby shower turned out to be a turning point in her journey. Fiona said, "The office threw me this fabulous baby shower, and everyone was just so incredibly welcoming and supportive of me being like them, a parent. Everyone wanted to talk about baby stuff." She said she had every reason to believe that Accenture would be supportive because of the personal support she had received from so many.

She explained that the domestic benefits topic became personal not just for her, but for others too: "It was a huge eye opener to me that parenthood was such a normalizing force. Becoming a parent, suddenly, did two things. One, it gave me that normalized access to all parents, which was empowering in itself. And secondly, I was now advocating not just for myself but on behalf of my family. And as a woman, that puts things in a different light. The shower was a turning point."

Think about the momentum builders you need in your change. Also, watch out for some potential traps. Make sure your momentum builders:

- Are aimed toward your bigger goal
- Aren't a distraction at the expense of higher priorities
- Are one step toward longer-term progress
- Are real and will be viewed as momentum builders in a few months, not just today

Momentum builders aren't all alike. It's important to consider the type that will be meaningful and helpful to your wave. The momentum builders you need in one situation may go unnoticed in another. Momentum builders may include:

Quantitative results. This may be a noticeable improvement in sales for your new store or product. It can be an uptick in participation, increased attendance at your events, or a noticeable decrease in costs. These momentum builders are quantifiable and hard to debate. Some in your community will need this quantifiable result to take notice.

In fact, Wave Maker Melisa Miller, EVP and president of Alliance Data Retail Services, said that an immediate improvement in financial results was a momentum builder, but she had to manage the good news. She said, "We hit our first financial goal very quickly. It started happening so fast that we had to ensure everyone remembered that we still had much more to do."

Confidence builders. Julie Porter was the Wave Maker who encouraged my company, as well as other companies, to jump into social media and blogging several years ago. She built momentum by encouraging us to take the first few steps and experiment. We were busy with clients, so her first step was asking us to experiment, with the hope that it would become a higher priority once we got going. That led to us having visible success and some fun with it. This confidence inspired us to keep the momentum up.

Start by asking, "What will increase the confidence of others about this wave?" In Julie's case, she knew that we were originally skeptical about investing time in social media because we didn't see our clients there yet and we had time constraints. She encouraged us to try with the hope of changing our perspective.

Positive word of mouth. As we discussed in chapter 4, "Trends and Your Wave," word of mouth is the most positive way to build momentum for anything, including your wave. A "Like" or a check-in tells your friends that you are active in a new group or are at your new favorite store. A personal recommendation, online or in person, does much more to engage our friends than any advertising or packaged promotion. Word of mouth is important, estimated to be behind 20 to 50 percent of all purchasing decisions.[3]

Think about how you share ideas with friends today. You informally share your suggestions for the best pediatrician, the ideal vacation destination, the best Italian restaurant, and recommend that new movie. You peruse social media to see what your friends and contacts are doing, reading, and watching.

I recently visited a new neighborhood restaurant with friends, and the owners had all hands on deck to make sure guests had a great first experience. As soon as my husband looked up for a refill of his water glass, the manager was there to ask if we needed anything. A friend had a mistake on her order and they didn't charge her for the meal. They offered free appetizers to those waiting. Their momentum builder was to create good word of mouth the first week. They knew from experience that positive word of mouth is essential for longer-term success in any business, but especially new restaurants.

Some companies think of first impressions as core to their business. A friend, Cindy Grossman, is director of first impressions (one of my all-time favorite job titles) at Mike Mills Wealth Management Company. The company realized that first impressions are an essential step in building a longer-term relationship and inspiring confidence in their customers.

Inevitability. Inevitability is based on quick progress that communicates that your idea and plans will be successful—so why not join in? Charley Johnson, Wave Maker and president of the Pay it Forward Foundation, said, "We just claimed the movement and let everyone know we were on our way to reaching our goals. We didn't sit back and wait."

Joe Nussbaum, creator of The Big Event at Texas A&M University, said that his team built momentum by talking to so many people that their idea became legitimate in a very short period of time. Their momentum builders consisted of multiple actions and conversations, but resulted in a feeling of inevitability.

Some momentum builders come as a surprise, but many can be addressed in planning or even created. I have been part of many large organizational changes that were designed around a few momentum builders. This gave the effort a positive first impression that helped build momentum.

> **"Let's face it, you don't have long."**
> —*Joe Nussbaum*

THINK TIME

1. Who do you want to notice your momentum builders? (customers, friends, recruits, team members, your new community built around your idea, etc.)
2. What kind of momentum builders will have the most impact in your situation?
3. List all your ideas for momentum builders that fit your change and situation.
4. What is within your control in terms of creating momentum builders?
5. List the momentum builders(s) to add to your plan.

CHAPTER 7

Creating a Community Around Your Wave

Your idea emerged and took shape with your Idea Partners. Now you are ready to expand the circle so that your wave lasts and is sustainable. Most true changes need a broader community of interest and involvement to thrive.

I use the word "community" to describe those who care about what you care about and who show it with their actions. A community is a group actively committed to the cause. It's made up of people who care, want the outcome that you want, and are involved in a hands-on way. Communities aren't created based on a job title or position. They are built around those committed to your wave.

Before you think, "I could never create a community around one of my ideas," let's take another look. Here are some examples of communities that enabled a wave:

- Those who supported a new charity that eased the fears of children diagnosed with diabetes
- An informal working group dedicated to improving process efficiency and, as a result, creating a better customer experience
- A group of parents with big ideas for improving the fine arts curriculum in their school district
- A neighborhood Bible study that changed the lives of the participants
- A women's networking group dedicated to mentoring, learning, and sharing

Communities are not just for experts or those with impressive titles. High school students have started groups to share wasted food with the homeless. There is a local retiree group that formed a community around their passion for Habitat for Humanity. A community has a purpose that matters and that takes more than one person to accomplish.

Tory Johnson is a Wave Maker, #1 *New York Times* best-selling author, business owner, and weekly contributor to *Good Morning America*. Her wave is helping women get what they want—from finding the right employment opportunity, to starting a successful business, to taking control of their health. Tory started Spark & Hustle conferences several years ago to encourage women and to let them share ways to grow their businesses. The surprise was how much they helped one another—a community was formed. Tory explained:

> We started using the term BBF—instead of 'best friends forever', you're 'business best friends'. What we've seen is rather than just a "you go, girl" camaraderie there's a real sense of, I'm going to be a champion for your business. I'm going to introduce you to a manufacturer, or a vendor, or I know someone who could benefit from your expertise, I'm going to make a referral. There's a real sense of genuinely supporting one another. And that's what happens when you get a lot of people in a room together and everyone wants to row in the same direction. That's taken me by surprise, partially because I've always been in a business that's about supporting women, promoting women. But I think sometimes there can be a sense of competition that if I help someone else, it could be at my own expense. But not in this community.

Here are the key ingredients for a successful community that will propel your wave forward:

1. Change that matters
2. Teams that care
3. Teams that share

CHANGE THAT MATTERS

Any lasting change is based on a purpose that is bigger than one person; it's a change that makes the community, work, family, or marketplace better for all.

Build Around an Idea People Care About

We have talked about the importance of true meaning throughout *Make Waves*. To last, a community must be dedicated to something bigger, a cause that matters today and that will matter tomorrow.

As Guy Kawasaki, responsible for marketing the first Apple Macintosh computer and a leading author and business advisor, said, "The key to creating a meaningful community is to create something worth building a community around."[1]

> "It's kind of like a moth to a flame. Create something that
> matters and people will come."
>
> —*Charley Johnson*

The Wave Makers I interviewed built their changes on values, a purpose, and meaning that connected a committed community to the cause. Their stories are based on a diverse mix of important causes, from a company culture change, to paying it forward, to changing the culture of a major league clubhouse, to respecting diversity. But the causes were all bigger than just one person.

Less WIFM and More WIFU

The classic rule of sales and influencing is to share the WIFM: "What's in it for me." I believe this to be true in general, but in the extreme it can place too much emphasis on self. Waves are a little different. You aren't looking for the quick yes so that your target will buy a product or approve the request. You are looking for more. You need to find WIFU: What's in it for *us*?

"What's in it for me" may help others get on board at first because they know it will give them something they value (more money, better hours, more support), but interest in that will fade over time. In a wave, you'll need to go one step beyond, to "What's in it for us"—as a community, organization, family, or world. If you remember to think about what's in it for us, you get to the bigger values and purpose that engage others to make our work, organization, and lives better.

> "If you focus on 'What's in it for me' you promote individual
> agendas and priorities. Go for the purpose that isn't dependent upon
> the extrinsic rewards."
>
> —*Rich Sheridan*

When Rich Sheridan redefined how teams created software at Menlo Innovations he changed almost everything. Rich said, "I reminded them why they chose this profession of developer to begin with. Sure, at the most basic level it's typing into a computer. But we chose this career to make something better. Over time in organizations people can lose that sense of purpose and they seek the extrinsic rewards to balance it out. We had to return to our purpose of why we were doing this work to begin with and find the joy in it again."

> "When you focus on the much bigger prize outside and bigger
> than the organization, no one complains about the coffee anymore."
>
> —*Rich Sheridan*

TEAMS THAT CARE

A wave needs people who care about the cause and who are committed to making it a reality. I always define commitment as what we do when no one is looking. A true change needs that kind of interest that goes well beyond compliance. If the team cares about the outcome, they will contribute and stay with you through setbacks and challenges.

Encourage Accountability

In chapter 2, "Think Like a Wave Maker," we talked about the importance of accountable members in any change. Accountable people ask, "What can I do?" and "How can I help?" They spend their energies on what's in their circle of influence. Even if you have just a small working group interested in getting your idea off the ground, you need accountable and committed participants ready to roll their sleeves up and help the cause.

Promote Collective Ownership

Collective ownership doesn't mean a free-for-all or a modern-day commune, but rather that community members are partners, not recipients. Everyone contributes sometimes and receives at other times, but everyone has a role to play. Communities may have a leader or organizer, but it isn't a command-and-control, hierarchical structure. All members think of themselves as "owners" and contributors. I love how Bob Wright, of Dallas Social Venture Partners, described people involved as "mothers and fathers" of the change.

> **"When we finished, we had a hundred mothers and fathers of the bigBANG!"**
> —*Bob Wright*

This idea that we are all contributors is emerging in our economy. As we discussed in chapter 4, the sharing economy is opening opportunities for individuals to share their assets. You can share your car, your office, or your apartment by the day. A sharing community shares what they have, usually at some profit in business, and everyone benefits. A community is a similar concept. It shares the assets and solves problems together.

Wave Maker Trisha Murphy Rae is the co-founder and executive director of Christmas is for Children. One of the organization's big events is the annual food basket assembly on the next-to-last Saturday before Christmas. The room bustles with energy and Christmas carols while hundreds of families and students enthusiastically load over a thousand holiday baskets. At my first event, the baskets were bursting with food and ready to go by noon, as planned. It was a big success.

Afterward, I mentioned to Trisha that I saw a few opportunities to make this amazing event more efficient and streamlined. Trisha said something then that stuck with me, "Yes, we probably could make it more efficient, but people like to feel as if they are part of it and have some ownership in what they work on. So, if we still finish on time a little bit of overlap or inefficiency may be okay."

As someone who studies and advises on organizational change, I had to pause, because she was so right. The trade-off for more efficiency, when we were meeting the objective, had more downside than benefit in this situation. She and the team had created an event that built commitment for not only the event but the cause. This organization is successful because so many people are invested in the Christmas is for Children community and the event—not as spectators but as participants.

I remember this story when I think of collective ownership, because optimum efficiency may come at the expense of letting others have a voice and a hands-on role. And the community that stays committed can do so much more than any single process change.

Collaborate with Intent

A community isn't made of spectators because a community works together to solve problems, realize goals, or make something better. It has a purpose. The collective ownership idea means that there are many voices, not just one. And it means that everyone contributes—there are no spectators.

I facilitated a leadership workshop recently, and we played word association with the word "collaboration." I wrote the words this leadership group shared on my flip chart:

- Slow
- Group think
- Can lack focus
- Inefficient

This group envisioned wandering meetings, fruitless brainstorming sessions, and input with no outcomes. If it's a basic task, process, or crisis, then, yes, "collaboration" may live up to all of these words. After this session, I decided that "collaborate" needs a PR campaign.

Collaboration is much more than asking everyone for their ideas. Productive collaboration needs a well-thought-out process and a purpose that is transparent to everyone. It doesn't happen by bringing a group together and asking them to join hands and collaborate. It is very intentional, with a desired outcome. Collaboration takes focus, guidance, a process, and oversight. Ask for input and collaboration where you need it, not on outcomes that are predetermined or nonnegotiable.

You'll also remember in many of the Wave Maker stories how they used collaboration to move their wave forward, even if progress seemed slower at first. While collaboration may seem inefficient in the beginning, if used properly it will benefit your wave over time and help build momentum.

Crowdsourcing and crowd funding are ways of collaborating. As we discussed in chapter 4, this is a growing trend that allows anyone to raise capital, solve a problem that one person would have handled alone in the past, or incorporate best thinking very quickly.

Demonstrate Mutual Respect

A community must value the participation and involvement of all members. If the community has people of all different roles, interests, and experience, this respect must extend to everyone who is involved. Again, we aren't talking about a hierarchical group.

Mutual respect implies a level playing field on importance of contribution. The powerful—by external standards—must be committed to being one of the group. Likewise, all members have a responsibility to speak up and participate.

Charley Johnson, of the Pay it Forward foundation, talked about the importance of being responsive to everyone. There are many groups that are part of the Pay it Forward community and, as a result, his team hears many ideas and suggestions. He said, "You can lose so much trust and commitment by not responding to people who want to be part of the community."

> **"You develop trust through complete transparency."**
> —*Clint Hurdle*

Trisha Murphy Rae, of Christmas is for Children, explained the importance of respecting everyone's talents and contributions, and especially valuing volunteers: "Find the strengths of the people who want to help. Some volunteers can't see their gifts and their talents. But help them identify their strengths and find where they can contribute and be part of making it all happen. It's important for you and your goals, the strength of the organization, and for the volunteers too."

Use the Magic of the Small Group

In chapter 4, "Trends and Your Wave," we discussed the growing importance of peer power. It is essential to consider when planning your wave too. If your change needs an active community of more than twenty-five to thirty people, consider how you can make it feel smaller. Commitment is more likely when we know our participation is needed.

Have you noticed, when you attend an event with more than about thirty people, that it's easy to be a spectator rather than an active participant? It's because the group is big enough that you can step safely to the sidelines, smile, nod, and go home. It's officially someone else's baby. But if you are in a discussion with five to ten people, your silence is noticed. Your opinions will be heard—they matter more. It's much harder to be a spectator in a small group. The size and scale need to be considered when you define your community.

There are many mega churches in Texas. My first reaction was, "How can you feel part of a group with ten thousand–plus members?" Yet, their members are connected to much smaller neighborhood groups, Bible studies, Sunday School classes, and discussion groups that are intended to make these massive memberships seem much smaller. Businesses do this too. Accenture has always had "start classes," so that new graduates are part of a smaller group, which lets them build camaraderie and help one another. Oracle does the same. Those relationships often last throughout careers because of the bond shared at a significant time.

A few years ago, when Wave Maker Julie Porter was in the early days of starting Front Porch Marketing, she used the small-group concept to perfection. She asked a diverse group of people she knew and trusted over to her house for dinner with the "ask" of giving her advice and ideas for starting her new business. Over wine and dinner there were new introductions and people catching up after too long. One guest helped another with a job connection and others discussed new business opportunities. Julie had pillows on the ground and flip charts in the corner of her living room. One friend acted as the facilitator. A few key questions were posed to the group on defining the company name, brand, and target market. We all left that night with some new or renewed business friendships, Julie had a great list of ideas for her new venture, and she had created an ad hoc community of people behind her business. She also started some great word of mouth based on who was involved and how it was created. It all began with a small group.

If your wave is big and, as a result, the community is big, remember the small group. Even if your wave is smaller, a small group may be your community and the engine behind your momentum.

TEAMS THAT SHARE

A community grows by people sharing the importance and value. In a vibrant community, team members take on the role of chief communicators and are advocates for the change. This happens when we believe in the cause and care enough to influence others to be supportive or get involved.

When We Care, We Share

You want your wave to catch on and be shared by others. Your idea becomes a wave as others care too and you build momentum as more people get involved. A growing community is essential to enabling your wave.

Sharing takes effort and time, and there are many competing demands for our attention. Know why people will care about your idea and how it helps. We talked about the importance of building your wave on values and what matters most. Connect these values to your stories and conversations.

Jonah Berger, author of *Contagious: Why Things Catch On,* says, "Naturally contagious content usually evokes some sort of emotion.... Emotional things often get shared. So, rather than harping on function, we need to focus on feelings."[2] Our feelings are tied to meaning, which we know is essential in any wave. If we do this, what will be different or better?

You'll remember that we talked about the importance of inevitability. One of the ways you can realize inevitability is if your wave is not only needed and important, but will solve future problems. It's current and relevant. We all want to believe that we are part of making the future better. If your wave delivers on that promise, then make that connection for everyone involved.

> **"Our goal was that this change would become pervasive and inevitable. That was success for us."**
>
> —*Kate Rogers*

Many of the Wave Makers I interviewed used informal, individual conversations to discuss their ideas. There are many benefits of this strategy, including that it shows you care about people's participation as well as the cause. They matter. I have found a significantly different result when I ask colleagues for their input and involvement via a group e-mail or in a big meeting versus when I ask one on one. It's much easier to care when two people talk with each other or there is some personal connection via media. This can be a critical element at the beginning in making your wave contagious.

What does your wave need to become contagious? If you are starting a blog that you hope will grow your business, know what your future readers care about and how they can get involved. If you plan to turn a business around, balance your metrics with the visible outcomes that others care about and want to realize. If you are starting a new business, think about what will make your future customers care about your plans.

Lois Melbourne, Wave Maker and co-creator and former CEO of Aquire, described how her company engaged its customers in new and unexpected ways in the beginning:

> We were still telling people what "www" was when we set up a web server with a "try before you buy" version of the product so that people could start testing it. We were working out of the house and yet people from all over the world were downloading the software and testing it with a thirty-day trial. At that point in time no one was giving away enterprise software. We were bucking the system. So people were testing it and they trusted it, and bought it because it worked. It built a network because people trusted the software and, as a result, they learned to trust us.

Aquire found a new way, at that time, to engage its customers and community by sharing their software, and that openness created both a personal connection and great word of mouth.

Translate with Stories

We've learned that people listen and engage more when a concept is translated into real-life stories. It becomes relevant and meaningful to us when we can picture it or see it in a new way. There are countless articles and books on storytelling, and most speakers and writers use stories to engage the listener or reader. Storytelling can translate strategies, analytics, and metrics into real-life relevance. It is also essential in a wave. It translates and illuminates "the why," builds commitment, and shows your passion. It also helps your wave spread.

Wave Maker Guwan Jones was so insightful in the way she shared the impact of diversity on patient care at Baylor Healthcare System. I asked her a few questions and she told me so many stories that helped me understand. Guwan said:

> If we have culturally diverse health educators, then they can influence the entire team. For example, if the physician, who isn't from the patient's culture, works with a health educator and understands some of the barriers for the patient, it can be considered up front. So the physician now understands that the closest pharmacy for this patient takes three bus trips. And can we

give her a ninety-day supply of medication? And if finances are a big concern, let's look at the $4 drug list at Walmart and try to find an option there. We'll also look at the communication. All of the paperwork is in Spanish, yes, but it may be university, formal Spanish, and it's confusing to the patient. If health-care providers understand the barriers, it can change how they interact with patients. Then it's no longer that the patient is noncompliant, it's just that it needed to be translated to their world and situation.

After Guwan's simple, real-life stories, I completely understand that diversity in patient care isn't a corporate program; it is all about direct patient care—her passion.

Painting a picture plays an important role in your wave, because when you communicate your plans it's essential to describe them in a way that connects to others. However, storytelling is a strategy, not an outcome in itself.

I watched a CEO talk repeatedly about the importance of storytelling, and he was actually pretty good at it—when he was in front of the room. He could tell stories, but the problem was that it was a performance. He didn't have the same ability to connect when he wasn't on the stage.

My other caution on sharing stories is that they can imply that a dazzling performance is enough. As we've talked about throughout *Make Waves*, the conversation and collaboration are where your wave gains traction. Telling meaningful stories is essential in one-on-one conversations, as in my discussion with Guwan Jones, not only in big meetings.

> **"Tell stories and make it real, but have your facts and be informed too."**
> —*Fiona Grant*

With the caveat that storytelling isn't just a dazzling performance, but is about translating meaning and relevant examples, stories can be helpful to:

- **Help others better understand the problem.** A Wave Maker told me a story about a desolate call center and the dejected people working there. Cynthia Young described her first visit to the center:

  > When I went out to the call center for the first time, it was clear that they were abjectly miserable. It just *felt* miserable. I tried to figure out, what am I feeling here? Is this a vibe, or the lighting in here, or what? It was all of the above. There were no windows. The walls were gray. The carpet was torn and soiled and gray. The cubicles were not decorated. There was a hush, even though it was a call center. It was

very, very quiet. There was no laughter. I started going around and meeting people, and they wouldn't look at me. As I walked down one aisle, one young guy was standing up with his headset on, and he was talking to a customer, kind of pacing back and forth. And when he saw me, he ducked down and dropped into his chair. When he finished with the call I went back around and asked if he was okay and he said, "Yes, I'm sorry. I'm sorry." I said, "What are you sorry for?" He responded, "We're not allowed to stand up."

As she told the story, I could picture it, and I quickly understood why she felt a call to action to change the culture there. Had I worked there, I would have been part of her change community. Just her stories made me get it and understand the importance.

- **Share an early success**. Tell how your change is impacting the customer or employees in ways beyond just the metrics. This is an important way to build momentum behind your change. In chapter 6, we discussed the need for momentum builders and shared that an early success can give your change a boost.
- **Inspire for the future**. A few years ago I contributed to planning an organization-wide change that affected almost everything and everyone—new processes, technology, roles, and ways of interacting with customers. Our strategy was to describe the new world once the changes were in place. We used storytelling to convey that the short-term pain would be worth it because tomorrow would be much better for everyone. They had to get a glimpse of it before they could see the potential.

Lori Myers, Wave Maker and president of Chase's Place School, said that one of her first actions in her new role as president of the school was to build more communications support. "We needed financial contributors, but we also needed people who contributed with their hands and their time. I had to find ways for others to see the good we were doing in this school. We used videos, visits, and personal stories to help others see what we saw."

> "Most people deep down want to help others and children in our community. I knew that if anyone walked into this school, met these children, and heard their stories, they would be committed to Chase's Place."
>
> —*Lori Myers*

Talk Straight

Straight talk is simple and authentic. In chapter 5, we reviewed the importance of simplicity in purpose and goal. Simplicity is critical to building interest in your wave and growing the community because it makes your change easily understood and the goals clear. In business, we can get sidetracked with overengineered language designed to impress more than engage and help others understand.

I like to use the "grandmother test." If your grandmother can't understand your wave, you have more work to do. Your grandmother is a great example, because she is not involved in your work and may not completely understand what you do! And, that is exactly why she is the perfect test case. Your message has to be so simple, clear, and compelling that your grandmother not only gets it but even finds it interesting.

Sometimes our fears, discussed in chapter 2, reappear when we share our ideas. Those fears that cause us to wonder, "Am I smart enough?" or "Are my ideas important enough?" can translate into "important" language designed to make us sound and feel significant. This can cause simplicity to take a backseat to complexity.

I love the book *Why Business People Speak Like Idiots* by Brian Fugere, Chelsea Hardaway, and Jon Warshawsky. It is a laugh-out-loud look at how business communication is drowning in jargon and buzzwords, along with some great ideas for how to fix it. The authors say,

> The average white collar worker goes to the office every morning and plugs into e-mail, dials into voice mail, and walks into meetings only to be deluged by hype and corporate speak:
>
> *After extensive analysis of the economic factors and trends facing our industry, we have concluded that a restructuring is essential to maintaining competitive position. A task force has been assembled to review the issues and opportunities, and they will report back with a work plan for implementing the mission-critical changes necessary to transform our company into a more agile, customer-focused enterprise.*"[3]

This would be hilarious if it weren't so true. If you work in a large organization, there is a good chance you live this every day. Some businesspeople use this jargon as naturally as they use their computers and their business casual wardrobe. As a Wave Maker, fight the urge to join in. Remember that your goal is to find meaning and connection and this language doesn't help you.

A few years ago I had a very natural and real conversation with a leader before an important meeting. He then excused himself to speak to his team in front of the large hotel ballroom. Suddenly, everything changed. How did this compelling, engaging human being turn into the corporate actor in front of the room? It comes from years of practice and an unconscious belief that this is what you are supposed to do. But it doesn't have to be that way.

Fugere, Hardaway, and Warshawsky identify four traps that keep us from communicating in real language: obscurity, anonymity, hard-sell, and tedium. I want to mention the hard-sell trap now, because when you start a wave you are trying to influence and convince, not to use the hard sell.

They say:

> We overpromise. We accentuate the positive and pretend the negative doesn't exist—not because we received our business training on used car lots, but because we are human, and we like to be optimistic. The result is that we do too much hard selling. This may work for those pushing Abdominizers on late-night television, hoping to sway a few clueless, lonely, or drunken souls. But, it's dead wrong for persuading (sober) businesspeople to listen. At the end of the day, people hate to be sold to, but they love to buy. With access to loads of information and instant communication, people today question everything. They know the hard sell and—with trust in business at an all-time low—even the slightest whiff of it sends people running for the exits."[4]

Where do you draw that line? Be positive and share the opportunity, but don't hide the challenges. The "shove it under the rug" strategy means that problems will reappear later with more power than ever. In a wave, you want to create momentum builders for your change, but totally unexpected problems can derail your progress. You are much better off being open about the risks, likely problems, and predicted bumps in the change. And it's important to remind yourself and others that when you experiment, there will be mistakes. Expect them.

I was involved in an acquisition, and at the start of the transition the most senior leader stood in front of the new employees and said there would be very few changes. "Just think of this as business as usual," he said. They were so relieved and pleased with this exciting news.

Yet there was no chance of that happening, given the business plan. As the weeks unfolded, more and more significant changes were introduced. This leader bruised his credibility and trust with this group so badly that he never recovered. He had gone for the easy answer in his very first communication and, as a result, he wildly overpromised. The employees learned drip by drip that he wasn't telling them the truth.

Wave Maker Melisa Miller, EVP and president of Alliance Data Retail Services, made many changes in her wave but not to the ultimate objectives. Her instinct was to be open and lay it all out, then get moving. She knew that if she and her team kept their communication simple and direct, the three thousand–plus employees involved in the change would understand the change and their role in it.

> "I'm a big believer in pulling the Band-Aid off at once and starting to move forward."
>
> —*Melisa Miller*

Everyone's wave is unique and different, yet all depend upon simple and honest communication to maintain the integrity of both the Wave Maker and the wave.

Meet Others Where They Are

As you start sharing your ideas and direction with a broader group, it's very easy to assume that everyone knows what you know. After all, you have been thinking about this topic for months or years. Now it's time to go back to the ground and remember that this broader group is new to your ideas. Newcomers will need time to absorb and catch up. Not everyone will want to get involved in the same way. If you miss these differences, your participants may lose interest. This disconnect can cause you to be impatient with others because they don't appear committed or may not show much interest.

Lindsay Pender, a Wave Maker, shared that she was driven to help premature newborns by what she had learned at her previous job at a metropolitan state-of-the-art hospital. At the same time, she knew that her fellow nurses at the new, smaller hospital needed time to understand and hear her perspective. She recognized that she was at a different starting point, so she was patient and open to others while maintaining her commitment to the desired change.

Pause to consider if your own style is a nice fit for this point or if you will have to adjust. This is a time when you are five steps ahead of your broader community, so you have to remember that you are in a different place. If you like quick action and are ready to go, this may be a challenge for you. You'll need to focus more on what your community needs to know than what you already know.

Mark Benton, a Wave Maker who redefined careers in R&D at PepsiCo, shared how he had to adjust his pace to stay in synch with others: "I had lots of ideas and plans, but I didn't bring out my all of my ideas at once. And that was a big learning that I had from one of my senior leaders. I knew all of the wonderful things

I wanted to do and I was planning to deliver them all at once. I got the advice to pace myself and not try to do everything at once."

> **"If you are running too far ahead and they can't see you, you have to adjust."**
>
> —*Melisa Miller*

Combine Enthusiasm and Substance

Eric Buhrfeind, a Wave Maker who created the partnership between Accenture and MIT for an advanced certification, said he depended on both enthusiasm and substance: "You have to have enthusiasm and passion combined with a lot of substance. You can't have one without the other or it won't work."

I once had a mentor tell me, "No one will ever be more enthused about your ideas than you are." A simple statement, but it has stuck with me. Bringing your wave to life takes optimism paired with a heavy dose of substance.

I have seen this important balance in my experience and over and over again in studying change and Wave Makers. I found that all showed enthusiasm in their own unique way. Some had energy and excitement in their voices when they shared their experiences, while others were quieter but exuded such confidence and belief in their wave. They were all very different people pursuing unique changes, but each shared an individual brand of enthusiasm and authenticity.

> **"Show enthusiasm in a way that is comfortable for you. Be yourself. Be authentic."**
>
> —*Julie Porter*

Julie Porter, CEO of Front Porch Marketing, shared how she persuaded clients to embrace social media as a natural part of their business: "You absolutely have to know what you are talking about, but it also takes enthusiasm and encouragement. When people are trying something new and experimenting, it's essential. And I think the importance of encouragement is often forgotten."

THINK TIME

1. What is the cause that matters in your wave?
2. How can you ensure that your wave is focused on "What's in it for us" rather than just "What's in it for me"?
3. How can you promote collective ownership?
4. What strategies can you use to promote accountability?
5. What is your natural style in communicating, and will you have to adjust to ensure you don't assume too much?
6. How can you connect stories to your larger purpose?
7. How natural is it for you to tell a story to illustrate and share meaning?
8. How can you improve your capabilities in telling stories and painting a picture of the need?

CHAPTER 8

When the Wave Comes to You

Waves can start in your imagination or they can begin when the phone rings with a surprising need or request. Sometimes a big change appears out of nowhere, and you are the one who must take it on, whether you wanted it or not. On the personal front there are many such changes—the loss of someone you love dearly, the move to a new city because of a transfer, or a surprise new addition to the family. Some bring sadness and others excitement, but these changes weren't things you planned.

At work, waves come to our doorstep often: a merger completely changes the company you put your heart and soul into, a senior leader personally asks you to take on a big priority, or your local community needs a movement to help the homeless. Your change began because it came to you or you saw a need you couldn't ignore.

Let's look at waves that come to you from two perspectives:

- Starting a wave that comes to you
- Contributing to a bigger wave

STARTING A WAVE THAT COMES TO YOU

Wave Maker Lori Myers is president of Chase's Place School, a school that began because public and private schools couldn't meet the needs of these children with disabilities. But being the president of Chase's Place School wasn't part of Lori's master plan. She explained:

Another couple started Chase's Place School in 2003, and we started my daughter there when she was just five years old. And then in 2010, the owners of the school decided that they could no longer continue, for many reasons. They had a meeting with a group of parents and they told us that they were planning to leave. As we were processing their decision, the next question was, "Would you guys like to take over?"

The parents there that day ultimately said, "Yes, we've got to do this." So, we talked and decided we just had to figure it out. There weren't any other options. There was no way we could realistically find the right place for our children in just a few months. So, we decided to put our heads together and keep this going.

Lori described how she naturally became a Wave Maker: She started off by committing to help the group and then somehow became president of the board. Lori didn't look for the wave. It came to her. She explained:

I kind of have this bad habit of taking over. I can't mind my own business. And I really didn't mean to do this because I have young children, one with special needs. And my initial reaction was, "How in the world am I going to manage this?" I'm busy! I don't have a lot of idle time. My fear was "How are we going to actually keep this going?" One thing I do feel like I'm good at is finding good people. And knowing what deficits I have and where we need to find experts. We now have the right experts and team in place. And I tried to put some business parameters in place. Cut costs, focus on the structure and the right priorities. I did everything I could to make our vision stay alive.

In this example, Lori's change was presented to her by someone else. Even when a wave isn't our idea we, like Lori, can ask, "What can I do?" and "How can I help?"

> "I knew I'd be successful and that I could do it.
> I just didn't know how yet."
> —*Mark Benton*

Here are some examples of waves that come to you:

- A leader asks you to take on a significant strategic priority
- Your friend asks you to join the board of a new nonprofit to support battered women, and you know that service is desperately needed
- You receive a call asking if you are interested in buying the neighborhood restaurant you've always dreamed of, even though it's sooner than you'd planned
- A personal situation requires you to start a new career or take on new responsibilities for your family

The difference between the wave you envision and the wave that appears in front of you is how and why it starts. When the wave comes to you, you are educating yourself on the current situation, how the wave or the request for the wave came about, and what can be done. And you need to decide if it is the cause you want to lead.

Kate Rogers, Wave Maker and leader at H-E-B Grocery, started a wave to make H-E-B a health and wellness destination. It began when the president of H-E-B asked her to take on this challenge and accelerate the company's progress. Kate was passionate about health, and she had started another wave at H-E-B, as she is also a vocal champion of childhood literacy and education. Because of her previous wave-making success and her commitment to health, she was asked to lead this enterprise-wide change.

Health and wellness was core to the H-E-B identity and brand. The company's leaders wanted customers and the larger community to see the stores as health destinations and they wanted buyers, employees, and store leaders to be committed to this cause in their stores.

Kate talked about how health and wellness can be a challenge for the grocery industry, because all types of foods are offered in stores, not solely healthy options. She said that it took extra education and reframing of the issue to show that H-E-B could be an advocate for health while still offering choices. Kate said, "We had created several task forces in the past and talked about a desire to be known for our commitment to health, but nothing had been successful. We weren't making enough progress. Health can be a scary topic in our business and a very personal topic. There was resistance in places even though we had leadership sponsorship. I took it on."

She built a coalition of people across the business who believed in promoting health and wellness, and they looked for ways to integrate it into everything they did. The team kicked off The Biggest Loser Challenge for company employees and it was so successful that they expanded it to involve customers. They experimented with new ways to share health information in stores that customers valued. In addition, the group educated H-E-B's leaders on their role in health and wellness and asked buyers to look for more healthy options for their stores. Kate and her allies talked to hundreds of people about their ideas.

Kate didn't ask for the wave, but she took it on enthusiastically when it came to her. When asked about her lessons learned, Kate said, "I would have asked more clarifying questions and gathered more information right up front to understand the definition of success. I usually jump into challenges quickly. I rarely have fears on this sort of thing. I only see the possibilities. Even though I believe nothing is impossible, it's still important to ask the right questions right up front so you understand expectations, get the resources you need, and know your options."

Size up your starting point before you commit. When a wave comes to you, there a few key questions to ask yourself:

1. Is there an opportunity to be successful?
2. What will it take?
3. What can I do?

Is There an Opportunity to Be Successful?

Wave Maker Kate Rogers, of H-E-B, sized up the situation and then got started. She took some short-term actions, like finding others who were committed, and started meeting with them more frequently. She looked for ways to build momentum for her wave. She had leadership support, the cause mattered, and with time others would become part of the health and wellness wave at H-E-B. Kate knew they would be successful.

Understanding your starting point is essential. Learn everything you can through research and by talking to experts or those previously involved. This assessment is important, so you understand what can be done and if you are positioned for success. Before you commit to the outcome, understand your starting point.

A friend we'll call Angie wanted to start her own business. She was approached by a successful business owner in her field who planned to retire, and he suggested she buy his business. Angie was thrilled that her dream of entrepreneurship was right in front of her and she wouldn't have to start from scratch. Her excitement built as she pictured herself hopping on the fast track to running a full-scale business. At her friends' urging, she took the time to ask an expert to conduct a thorough business assessment. She soon learned that the business's profit had trended downward the past three years and that a client that represented over half of the company's revenue was due to a close relationship with the current owner. At first, it seemed like a once-in-a-lifetime opportunity. But, after pausing and reviewing the analysis, she reluctantly concluded that the business wasn't a wise investment for her. But, if she hadn't taken the time for a proper assessment she might have acted too soon, just because the opportunity appeared in front of her.

What Will It Take?

Assess what it will take to start and sustain the change. You have to determine if you are able to start this wave.

Mark Benton, Wave Maker and a senior director at PepsiCo, was asked to develop a strategy and plan for growing careers in Research and Development.

Mark knew that there were many expectations and opportunities. His first step was to make sure he understood the problem to solve. He said, "I listened and gathered information. Given the expectations, I knew I had to move quickly. So I borrowed what had worked well in other groups and used best thinking. I also created new ideas that fit R&D. I had an important core group of people who were there with me and they became ambassadors for the change."

Mark quickly sized up "what will it take," and used creativity and a practical approach to make progress. He also realized that he had to approach the global change in phases. He didn't have the option of waiting until everything was complete before introducing the completed R&D career model and new program.

Mark said, "One of my biggest lessons was the importance of phasing and pacing, not just for me and my team but for the organization. There was a limit to what could be absorbed at one time. Don't share everything you have at once."

What Can I Do?

When a wave comes to you, you have to answer carefully the question "What can I do?" You may not have started with a passion for the idea or it may have arrived when you weren't quite ready. That initial lack of preparedness changes how you think about it. You have already decided whether there is an opportunity to be successful and you've identified what it will take. Now, you have to decide if you are the one.

If you are asked to take on the leadership for an important wave, like Kate and Mark were, you will likely begin with how to get it started. But, even in those situations, it's important to understand the definition of success and ensure you are aligned with leadership on your approach. These up-front conversations are essential to making sure that you can deliver what is expected.

Earlier in my career, I was asked to take on a leadership role in building our global services business, which was a very big change in strategy for our organization. I found the work content interesting and I was enthusiastic about the new challenge. However, at the time our two boys, Will and Patrick, were young and there was a limit to how much global travel I was willing to do. So, right up front, I shared my personal boundaries and let my leadership know that if I took on the role, I'd have to be creative so that I could limit my travel. I was clear that for it to work, I would have to do it my way. They agreed. And that was an important part of deciding if and how I could take on the responsibility.

And, much like the earlier example about the business up for sale because of a retirement, someone else's timing might not be yours. Not every opportunity to lead a wave will be suited to you or appear at the right time. I hope you have learned from *Make Waves* that a wave requires passion and a tireless commitment to the cause. If you don't have that desire or time, then you may need to decline or find a creative alternative, such as partnering with others or finding a good co-leader to head the wave with you.

> "If you start losing the passion, the magic potion is gone. The minute you lose the passion, you've got to reevaluate."
>
> —*Kathy Korman Frey*

THINK TIME

1. How does the wave match up with your passions, values, and interests?
2. Is there an opportunity for success? How do you know?
3. What will it take to be successful?
4. What role can you play in the success?
5. Why are you prepared to lead it?
6. What creative options exist for starting the wave that involve others?
7. What impact can you have by leading the wave?

CONTRIBUTING TO A BIGGER WAVE

We are all contributors to changes around us at work, in our communities, in our schools, or in our families. In fact, this role as a contributor can be as important as starting or leading a change. Anyone who starts a change needs you. And, you may be starting your own wave while contributing to others. We all wear a contributor hat.

Let's look at how you can be a valuable contributor to the wave that comes to you. We return to the main themes of this book, asking "What can I do?" and "How can I help?" And, as we discussed in chapter 2, building those accountability muscles and focusing on what is within our control and influence are critical, even when the wave isn't one you conceived of. With that mind-set, let's look at some key actions you can take to be an important wave contributor.

Being a Critic Keeps You on the Sidelines

Being a critic isn't difficult. It's pretty easy to find what's wrong even if you don't know anything about the topic. It's the best tactic for staying on the sidelines and keeping the responsibility squarely on someone else's shoulders. This point has never been made more eloquently than by former president Theodore Roosevelt:

It is not the critic who counts; not the man who points out how the strong man stumbles, or where the doer of deeds could have done them better. The credit belongs to the man who is actually in the arena, whose face is marred by dust and sweat and blood; who strives valiantly; who errs, who comes short again and again, because there is no effort without error and shortcoming; but who does actually strive to do the deeds; who knows great enthusiasms, the great devotions; who spends himself in a worthy cause; who at the best knows in the end the triumph of high achievement, and who at the worst, if he fails, at least fails while daring greatly, so that his place shall never be with those cold and timid souls who neither know victory nor defeat.

This is a good passage to post on your desk for inspiration when the temptation to be the critic is too great.

I've always used this key coaching point for those on my team who have aspirations of taking on more responsibility and a bigger role. You have to be more than someone who points out problems: you need ideas and actions for solving, changing, or innovating. One of my favorite leaders at Accenture, Don Monaco, always listened to our problems and concerns, and then ended with, "So, what's your recommendation?" I learned very early that if you see problems you better bring some recommendations too. Think about offering solutions rather than just pointing out what's wrong.

Critics can certainly wield power, especially over those who lack confidence in themselves or their ideas. If you want to be a valued contributor or trusted leader, leave this mind-set behind, unless you review movies or restaurants. This doesn't mean that you don't see the problem—you do—but assess it and quickly move on to what to do.

We can get stuck admiring the problem when we are presented with a change that flies against our assumptions and conventional wisdom, especially if it's a change we wouldn't have chosen. When you see problems, move quickly to ideas and solutions.

> "There will be naysayers and critics. You have to find the way to move forward anyway."
> —*Julie Porter*

Educate Yourself

When a change is introduced to you, it's unlikely that you are already the expert. Before you jump to your point of view and action, get some facts. Learn about the new change, whether it's moving to e-content and away from standard textbooks at school, launching a new mobile strategy, or converting to a completely virtual workforce. Quickly gather information about what other groups are doing, the latest trends, and success stories. It's hard to be a credible contributor or offer ideas with limited knowledge.

On a recent client project, the CEO shared his strategy to be less rules driven and to place more emphasis on improving service by granting employees and teams greater authority to operate, given set principles and desired outcomes. We were there to develop a series of actions for their leaders. A recent college graduate on the client team took immediate action. She started researching other organizations in the industry that used this strategy, signed up for a relevant conference, and shared articles and ideas. This was a great example of a team member immersing herself in the topic and sharing what she learned with her team. She had the mindset of a contributor, not a bystander.

Find the Gap

Take an objective look and determine where help is most needed. If the change is in the early stages, you may be an Idea Partner who can help shape the core idea. If it is further along, you may be someone who can help create part of the plan or engage others through positive word of mouth.

A friend of mine is an entrepreneur who has built a real estate firm. She said that the company's needs change from month to month based on priorities and growth. The gap isn't in one area, so she values people who are "utility players" and can adjust to the firm's changing needs. Quickly size up the gaps before you identify where you can best contribute.

> **"You have to fill a gap. If you're very good at picturing and visualizing the landscape that exists, you can look for the gap. Then, you can see how to fill it."**
> —*Kathy Korman Frey*

Know What You Bring to the Party

The ideal is when your strengths match the needs. We all have our talents, and we have the most impact when we know what we bring to the party.

In StrengthsFinder 2.0, Tom Rath shares the importance of using your unique talents: "When we're able to put most of our energy into developing our natural talents, extraordinary room for growth exists. So, a revision to the 'You-can-be-anything-you-want-to-be' maxim might be more accurate: You cannot be anything you want to be—but you can be a lot more of who you already are."[1]

I previously hired someone for my team who had perfect experience in operational leadership and had wonderful client relationship skills. But there was one problem: he had to contribute to some big changes in the organization, and he didn't understand the culture or the business well. He was too new, with limited knowledge of our industry. So, a first step was to identify a key team member to act as the perfect balance for him and help with his blind spots.

Lori Myers, Wave Maker and president of Chase's Place School, shared that she had no choice but to depend on others. She had business and organizational skills, but needed others to balance her limited educational and marketing expertise. She knew what she brought to the party, and those skills were essential in preparing her to be successful.

Use Your Intrapreneurial Skills

Intrapreneurs behave like entrepreneurs, but while working inside a large organization. In other words, intrapreneurs are people who have entrepreneurial talents but use them inside an organization and within a broader change.

In a recent *Forbes* article, David Armano, executive VP of global innovation and integration at Edelman, explained the growing appeal of the intrapreneur: "An intrapreneur is someone who has an entrepreneurial streak in his or her DNA, but chooses to align his or her talents with a large organization in place of creating his or her own. To the classic entrepreneur this may be puzzling, but to what I think is a growing class of 21st Century 'employees', it may sound like the best of both worlds."[2]

Organizations need ideas and creativity that contribute to bigger waves and change—that's where you come in. As we discuss in chapter 10, organizations that encourage and reward creativity, risk taking, and even failure greatly increase the likelihood of significant innovation.

Armano adds, "Smart organizations will seek out individuals who like to invent, innovate, and want to be on the front lines of change. These individuals can work independently but even more importantly can work seamlessly as part of an integrated team structure and also effectively embrace and embody the culture of the intrapreneur's host organization."[3]

Find your inner intrapreneur and bring your ideas to the table. The change needs you.

Incorporate Your Change into Your Day Job

Contributing to a wave through your day job can be as simple as asking yourself and your team, "What does this change mean for us?" and "How can we incorporate this change into our work?"

In my early years at Accenture there was a big emphasis on globalization. While the firm originated in the United States, it had become a global business. The CEO and his team had to remind the dominant U.S. leadership, at the time, of this essential and strategic change. I participated in an important meeting at which a colleague introduced recommendations for a new global program, after months of analysis and development. One big problem. He and his team hadn't involved anyone outside the U.S. to gather input, experiment, or review their recommendations. He confidently shared that the program was ready for approval and implementation. This did not go well. And, as my grandmother used to say, "You could see that train coming around the bend." He listened to the change message everywhere and yet went right back to his "business as usual."

It can be easy to think of the change as someone else's problem. Yet, at first, your contribution can be as simple as discussing implications within your team, identifying what needs to change, or even just tacking a Post-it note reminder above your desk. One of my clients is continuing to create a safety culture that goes beyond safety measures and metrics. As an example, one of their employees keeps a picture of his grandson on his phone as a reminder of the importance of safety. He won't forget.

Start a Ripple

We have mentioned the power of ripple effects throughout *Make Waves*. These begin with small decisions and actions within your control that propel the bigger change. Don't let your hurdle be too high. Go for the small things that you can do to help give the bigger wave momentum.

Here are a few examples of people performing small acts that can start a ripple:

- The manager who takes time to write personal notes of appreciation to her team and colleagues to keep interest up during periods of long and sometimes difficult change.
- The Parent Teacher Organization president who changes parent meetings to evenings, after the principal emphasizes involving both parents in education. She also suggests involving dads as classroom volunteers.
- The product developer who changes the development process to involve customer discussion groups much earlier, as part of a strategy to be more customer centric.
- The R&D scientist for a food and beverage company who sets up regular lunches with the nutrition team leader to encourage communication and coordination given their shared goals of developing more nutritious options.

Find even small changes that you can make today to contribute to the bigger goal. Remember to ask, "What can I do?" and "What can I influence or control?"

You can make a significant contribution even when the wave comes to you or you are part of a bigger change.

THINK TIME

1. What can you do to ensure that you move beyond problems and look for ideas and answers?
2. What do you need to learn to better contribute to the change in your organization?
3. What are the biggest needs in the organizational change?
4. What talents do you bring that can help make the change happen?
5. How can you use your intrapreneurial skills to develop new ideas?
6. How can you incorporate the new change into your day job and daily activities?
7. What actions can you take that will start even small ripples and help the bigger change in your organization or community?

CHAPTER 9

When Your Wave Hits a Wall

Not every wave will work. Some will never get started or, if they do, never build the momentum or reach the result intended. For all of the success stories, I also heard: "I couldn't get others interested," "It was a great idea, but there wasn't funding for it," or "In spite of my best efforts, I could never get my business off of the ground." And almost every Wave Maker told me of setbacks and problems they faced.

We all have failures. Every one of us. That is how we learn, grow, and get better. Failures can also be our best opportunities to learn. I bet if I asked you to list the times in your life when you learned the most, you'd have failures or some difficult times on your list. I know I would. And, that is the point—learn from your experience before you decide what to do next.

There isn't a one-size-fits-all answer. There's no guaranteed advice as simple as "Be persistent and keep going!" Likewise, a setback isn't a reason to say, "I'm done." At times like this, stay open-minded about why you hit a roadblock. Gather information and see where it leads you. Learn from your obstacle first and do some simple analysis before you decide your next step, much less give up.

Cynthia Young, a Wave Maker who changed the culture at her organization, said, "You have to be willing to make room for the possibility that you missed something. It doesn't mean your overall plan or what you're trying to accomplish is wrong. It just means that you might have to change tactics, not strategy. Not everything is going to have your ideal neat, happy ending."

> "It's important to know that not everything that you do is going to turn out just right."
>
> —*Cynthia Young*

Your overall objective is to determine whether you've hit a real brick wall or just a setback. There is a big difference. As I researched those who started waves, I realized that one of their distinguishing factors is that they are able to size up an obstacle, adjust, and work through it. As we discussed in chapter 2, Wave

Makers' focus on impact rather than personal recognition makes the setbacks less significant.

Wave Maker Charley Johnson, president of the Pay it Forward Foundation, shared his view on persistence: "The difference between those who are successful and those who aren't is that the successful just won't give up. When times got tough and everyone else would've given up, that is when they step up. And, I've challenged myself: do I honestly believe this is going to work? I'm just going to give up. And that's when I realize, no, this is exactly what I've always wanted."

Persistence is a prized virtue of those who start changes. Yet, persistence doesn't mean you plow ahead with your blinders on when your plan clearly isn't going to work. It's best to regroup and find another path that will. And there are times in life when our amazing idea looks very different in the rearview mirror. Accept that possibility.

> **"I think that in many cases it just boils down to plain old persistence."**
> —*Kate Rogers*

In this chapter, we'll use tools to help you assess whether you have a setback or a wall and give you the wisdom to know the difference. Each roadblock is different, so think about your situation; after reflection you'll have new insights. I also think this type of assessment is valuable for any setback you experience that involves others.

YOUR OWN DIAGNOSIS

A diagnosis is the identification of the nature and cause of a condition. A diagnostic is a method for drawing conclusions. After your doctor conducts tests, you may have a diagnosis of strep throat. My sons were given a diagnostic to determine their readiness for the advanced math curriculum. They provide a way to assess the facts, as well as rule out other options. Now it's time to turn that analysis on ourselves.

While it may be difficult to do, it's essential that you lift up and look at your situation from the third-person point of view. Step away from your personal feelings and your disappointment. Forget the second-guessing. Use whatever metaphor works for you: reporter, researcher, or business analyst. Pretend that you have no involvement in the situation and look at the facts objectively. It's also wise to seek some outside input and perspective. It can be difficult to assess on your own why something didn't work.

In this analysis, focus on the facts and real information, not your assumptions. Set aside your personal fears, your frustrations with others, and any feelings of unfairness. All of these blur the picture and keep you from clarity.

A few years ago I led a global change initiative. A key sponsor changed the expectations and desired outcome very late in the game, and her new strategy caused a significant last-minute adjustment. My team was in disbelief as we discussed the change, which came after months of work and just before a widely communicated launch date. I told them we had one night to be frustrated and angry. But the next morning all energies were to be spent on how we could adjust our plan. We all had our frustrations, but we had to leave them outside the door before we could decide what to do next.

After setting aside your frustrations or disappointment, it's time to analyze why your wave didn't have the impact you had planned.

Assess the Situation

This assessment is intended to help you determine what actually happened and why. Consider these key questions to encourage you to set aside your feelings and ensure you have a good grasp on the facts.

1. **What was your original objective?** Remember the original intent when you envisioned your wave. Return to the vision and why you believed it would make a difference.
2. **What were your actual results?** Consider objectively what happened, not your feelings about it. Focus on the facts and note the real results. What was happening when you made progress and, likewise, when you hit the roadblock? Be the researcher and look at what actually happened.
3. **What feedback did you receive from others on your idea?** What feedback did you receive and from whom? We know you can't expect consensus on a new idea or wave, but the feedback you received is important. What was the input from your core Idea Partners?

   It's important to separate who gave the feedback from what they actually said. Was there a difference in feedback on the idea versus the implementation? The person who gave you the input may determine the relevance. Were your naysayers professional naysayers who thrive on poking holes in any new idea from anyone? Did they have a personal bias that runs counter to your change? As an example, if you had resistance from a key person who values efficiency above all else, then she may not be interested in experimentation, even if it will help in the long run.

   There are some waves that require agreement from your boss. If she didn't agree, think carefully about the factors that affected that decision—timing, viability, cost, or need. Consider that carefully before deciding "It didn't work."

> "You should listen to as many people as possible. But if someone tells you "You shouldn't do that," you shouldn't just stop. Because people will."
>
> —*Allen Stephenson*

4. **What progress was made, even if you didn't realize ultimate success?** Have you noticed that when we discuss lessons learned we often go straight for the problems? It's easy to say, "I didn't explain my idea well enough in that key meeting," "I didn't have a good enough prototype," or "I should have experimented before I got leadership involved." All these thoughts are important, and may be true—but what worked well?

   I have had many situations where my idea/plan/change didn't quite gain traction at first but I knew I was building support to benefit the cause the next time. One leader told me that his wave didn't work on his first attempt, but he was a lot smarter and he'd know what to do next time. Recognize your progress and decide how it can work for you in the future.

5. **What didn't work as you had hoped?** Identify the disappointments or breakdowns that you haven't already considered. Think about the forces that worked against you no matter how small. Examples might be:
   - The expected sponsor who stayed on the sidelines
   - The big kickoff event that had to be rescheduled, which hurt momentum
   - The meeting where it became evident that not all of the costs had been considered
   - The pilot that created some mistrust in the product
   - The interview for the dream job that just never clicked

6. **What made your wave stop?** Summarize in one or two sentences what made your wave miss. Know the simple answer to this question, then break it apart to see what you can learn. This isn't about how you are feeling; it's about what actually happened.
   - If your funding was cancelled, why was it cancelled? Was it because of the viability of your project or due to other business issues?
   - If a key sponsor wasn't on board, why? Was it the concept or how it was presented?
   - If your new business didn't reach your first-quarter minimum goal, was your target too aggressive? What progress was made in that quarter that may impact the next one?

Set your personal feelings aside and determine the actual facts that let you know how and why you had hit a roadblock. Your answers to the questions above will help you understand whether your difficulties are a setback or a wall. A mentor often reminded me of an important point: "No answer isn't the same as 'no.'" I think of that when my first reaction is that I've hit a roadblock.

Determine What You Can Influence

You've now looked at the situation, and it's time to separate what you can control or influence from the issues outside your control. This is a return to the Circle of Influence referenced in Stephen Covey's 7 *Habits of Highly Effective People,* a leadership classic. Covey outlines the difference between our Circle of Concern (what we care about) and the Circle of Influence (what we can affect).[1]

The vast majority of people focus too much time and energy outside their Circle of Influence, in their Circle of Concern. Such people typically worry about things they can't influence much less control, such as the weather when they go on a beach vacation or who will become the new leader of their group.

Covey notes that highly effective people think and act primarily within their Circle of Influence. They set aside those things over which they have no control, and instead focus their time and energy where they can actually make a difference. They get to the "What can I do?"[2]

Even on matters over which you have no control or direct influence, you can still go back to "What can I do?" As an example, if your organization selects an outside hire for your new leader rather than the mentor you've known for years, you'll be disappointed. If you simply ask, "What can I do to improve my likelihood of success with the new leader?" you'll come up with a long list of ideas. It may include everything from setting time to meet her in person, learning about her previous company for information on its approach and culture, or identifying actions for sharing background information she will need. Even in situations that you don't control or influence, you can still identify positive actions to take.

You will remember that in chapter 2 we talked about the importance of accountability and that Wave Makers live in the world of "What can I do?" This assessment is intended to pull out what you can influence or control.

1. **How credible was your idea?** I'm using a very broad definition of the word ' "idea." It may be a business concept, a process change, a new book, or a new program. This question can be one of the hardest to answer when you are attached to it. But try to step back and look at it. Some questions to consider:
   - What need or gap did it fill?
   - What was the real impact of your idea?

- How much research did you do?
- What facts guided you to the idea?
- What experimentation or testing was done?
- How did you know the idea was meaningful?
- What made you believe it would work?

2. **Did you develop Idea Partners?** This question is to determine if the idea was able to gain traction with others who want what you want. Did you find interest in part of the idea, but not all? What resonated and what didn't? This question helps you determine if it is the idea that needs to be reconsidered, the way it was shared with others, or the execution.

3. **Who did you share your idea with?** Consider who you approached for their input or buy-in. What was their perspective? Did you discuss your ideas with those essential for making it work?

   You may have heard the story of J.K. Rowling, author of the Harry Potter series, the most successful book series in history, being rejected by at least twelve publishers because her manuscript was either never read or because "320 pages is far too long for a children's book." In Rowling's case, her book was rejected by many publishers, but it wasn't rejected by *every* viable publisher. She knew she just needed one. Her persistence kept her going to the next option and the next one.[3]

   Bob Wright, Wave Maker and creator of the bigBANG!, said that his persistence helped him, but hurt him in some ways too. He knew that he strained some relationships and stretched the trust he had built too far at times. He said, "There were definitely times that some people felt the honeymoon was over."

4. **Did you share your idea with both enthusiasm and substance?** We've already talked about the importance of marrying enthusiasm with the substance of your wave. Now it's time to objectively determine if you were able to do this.

   As Julie Porter, founder of Front Porch Marketing, said in her quest to get her clients to really engage in social media, "I had to adjust my style based on who I was talking with. Some need business rationale and others need more encouragement and enthusiasm. I always had both, but I relied more on one or the other based on who I was talking with."

   Storytelling is a way to build enthusiasm and let others know the substance or reality behind your change.

5. **How did others contribute to your idea?** Did you let others be part of shaping your idea? Did you get input from those who had knowledge you didn't have? One of the keys of a successful wave is to have

Idea Partners, but also to realize where your knowledge gaps are and where you need others. If you don't, you will hurt the credibility of your idea.

In my experience with global organizations, one of the fastest ways to hit a wall is to take a success from the United States and turn it into a global program with no input from colleagues around the world. No program works globally without input and involvement from multiple countries, no matter how good it is.

> **"I viewed a setback as a badge of honor."**
> —*Trisha Murphy Rae*

6. **Did you have the credibility and knowledge to be the visible leader?** Were you as informed as you needed to be? Did you gather the knowledge needed to develop and share your ideas? Also, a key point in this question is "to be the visible leader." Were you the best one to be in front, to share and recommend? Would someone else have been in a better position or had more credibility on the topic?

   Research tells us that change that lasts needs credibility. And we see that reality all the time. Have you ever experienced the phenomenon in a meeting where one person shares an innovative idea and there is no real interest, then a few minutes later someone else says essentially the same thing and everyone's eyes light up? Me too. In fact, this happened recently, and a friend sitting close by whispered to me, "Isn't that what I just said?" There are lots of reasons—some fair and some not—why this happens. But who brings up an idea, and when, does matter.

   I spoke with a recent college graduate who concluded that in her organization she needed a more senior sponsor to help her ideas gain traction because she was so new to the organization and the business. And, if her idea was about starting notable changes inside the organization, her assessment was probably accurate. It was more than she could do alone.

7. **How prepared were you for implementation?** This is a huge question listed here among the others. In fact, for most ideas execution is everything. Execution is what turns an idea into a wave.

   However, if you made it to implementation, you likely made progress. Of course, the reality comes in the "how." Conventional wisdom and research tell us that the majority of strategies fail at implementation. I actually believe that is true. Often, there isn't just one reason for the failure: implementation has many elements, and it will take an assessment to determine what worked and what didn't.

Organizations and people can create implementation conditions that make it very difficult for any waves to take hold. For example:

- **There are too many priorities.** Leaders identify twenty-five top, key, important, essential initiatives for the year. There are so many priorities that none of them rises to the top. Or an entrepreneur launches two or three businesses simultaneously and confuses his audience and Idea Partners.

- **The leader is an idea machine.** His ideas become the flavor of the day/ week/month. I once worked for a leader with this profile. It was understood within his team that you didn't act on every idea because he might not even remember it the next day.

- **The organization is ruled by the strategy of the day.** There are constant and dramatic changes in strategy or direction. I have seen leaders addicted to the next new thing and, as a result, priorities are always written in pencil. This can make a wave challenging because it's harder to tie to a bigger purpose. Also, it makes it harder to get traction because the unspoken view among the team is that "this too shall pass."

These factors can affect implementation success, yet they are not a reason to assume you can't make progress. These are conditions that require special planning on your part, to assess how to make progress when systemic, unsupportive forces are at play.

Wave Maker Mark Benton said he learned the power of a slow release by introducing changes step by step. In Mark's view, there is a limit to how much change people can absorb at one time. Pacing can be an essential element in a successful implementation. Consider whether the speed of new changes was a factor for you.

> **"Don't make a bigger meal than they are going to eat."**
> —*Mark Benton*

8. **What else was within your control in your wave?** Identify anything else that you had control over that affected your outcome or contributed to your setback, so that you can factor that into your Plan B.

Identify What's Outside Your Control

The other side of the coin is what's outside your control. Identify the factors that affected your progress but that you had no control or influence over. These are the rocks in your path that were just there. One of my favorite phrases is, "It is what it is," and sometimes we have to just accept that the situation isn't going to change and move on.

Make a list of the issues that affected you but were outside your control. And push yourself a little here to be sure that these things really *were* beyond your control.

As an example, I coached an executive who wanted to be promoted to the top position in his division. In exploring his current behaviors and goals, he explained, "I'm more of an introvert, so I'm not interesting or comfortable in front of big groups. I need to stick to smaller settings or written communication." As a result, he avoided being in front of his entire team and asked others to step in for him. His lack of visibility and his discomfort with sharing his views were interpreted by his team as a lack of interest or confidence. Yet, one on one he was very engaging, with a real passion for their work.

He had to change if he wanted to reach his goal of successfully leading his division. We created a plan to help him become more comfortable, but the plan reflected his own authentic way of doing things. He had to learn to interact with a bigger group just like he did in smaller settings or one on one. This executive also developed his speaking skills, because we explored the connection between his visibility and his success. So, we looked for what he *could* do, though his first reaction was that this was out of his control.

Here are a few questions to consider when looking at what's outside your control:

1. **Was timing a factor?** Timing can have a big impact on the success of any wave. If your wave appeared at the same time that your company faced a major market setback, it may not matter how great your idea is. Or, if you asked for funding a month after the annual budget was set, in some organizations you missed the window. In these situations, the quality of the idea or even the opportunity may not matter at this moment—maybe two months or a year later, but not today.

   Many entrepreneurs, especially in certain industries, were hit by recent changes in the economy. Some had to leave their dreams of a new business behind because of it. Even if they could have made changes to their plan, in some industries the timing was a major factor.

2. **How did financials or budget affect your progress?** Budgets and funding can be the difference between progress and a stall. In your situation, determine the impact of limited financial support. It's important to determine the impact of funding on your idea. Was it nonexistent or too limited to realize your goal? And was this completely outside of your influence?

3. **Did conflicting priorities affect your progress?** I had a leader tell me that his idea was needed and important, but the business was growing dramatically, so there were too many other priorities. They were working tirelessly to honor current client commitments but didn't have adequate resources. His idea was important, but in it was direct competition with other critical priorities. As a result, his change was never fully considered. There was little he could do to change the circumstances at that time.

Develop your Top Five Conclusions

What does your analysis tell you? If you were a writer, what would your first paragraph be? If you were a researcher, what conclusions would you reach?

You'll remember that in chapter 1 we outlined that a wave:

1. Creates undeniable impact at the right time
2. Has a bigger purpose that engages others
3. Is built upon knowledge and credibility

Now, with your researcher and reporter hat on, what does your analysis tell you about why your idea hit a wall or stalled? Think objectively about this before you create your new game plan.

I recently spoke with a friend who has been dreaming of a career change for several years. She wasn't sure that she could do it. She had marketable skills, but they weren't translating to actual interviews. So she assumed that a new job must not be in the cards, and was beyond disappointed. Together, we put on our researcher hats and looked at the facts objectively. She discovered that she had been far too dependent on applying online and had neglected consistently connecting to her personal and professional network. She "didn't want to burden them by asking for help." My friend concluded that, while she had a strong résumé, as well as the skills and abilities to make a career change, she hadn't engaged her Idea Partners and supporters. She concluded that her vision still worked, but she had to change the way she executed it.

What is your assessment? When ideas don't turn into waves, it's essential to step back and ask, "What are the facts telling me?" Many of us go to an answer too quickly based on our fears, assumptions, or just fatigue. And, sometimes, when the immediate answer is "It won't work" or "I'm not the one to do it," the assessment isn't accurate. Remember, Wave Makers are both persistent and flexible. They don't give up easily and adjust when they need to do so. They find the path after opening many doors, as there is usually more than one way to succeed.

CREATING PLAN B

Plan B isn't failure. It's simply a revised approach. In my experience, we often look back at Plan B and realize it was the better way all along, even if we didn't see that at the time. When you know that you need to go to Plan B, you essentially have four options:

- Change your idea
- Change your plan
- Change you
- Pause

The most important favor you can do for yourself is learn from your setback. Allow yourself to accept what needs to change and, most importantly, what you can do.

As Tory Johnson, Wave Maker, bestselling author, entrepreneur, and *Good Morning America* weekly contributor, said in a recent communication, you have to look in the mirror: "Too frequently a situation looks like this: You're repeatedly contacting the same five people who've expressed lukewarm interest. You're calling, texting, e-mailing, sending smoke signals—and in return you're getting absolute silence. The obvious conclusion that most people falsely make: NOBODY is interested. This just doesn't work. It's very easy to blame them—and to get angry at their refusal to respond—but that serves no constructive purpose and certainly won't generate business for you."

This is when you have to ask yourself if your message has meaning for your audience. Have you displayed both enthusiasm and substance? Does the timing fit your timetable or theirs?[4]

Focus on the things you can control. You have the responsibility to course correct or develop a Plan B when Plan A isn't producing the desired results.

Wave Maker Trisha Murphy Rae, co-founder of Christmas is for Children, explained that she viewed setbacks as part of doing something important: "I've always subscribed to the philosophy of 'Some will. Some won't. So what. Next,' and you just move on. Keep going and go to Plan B."

And, most of us can think of situations when we were hitting our heads against the wall trying to make Plan A work, when Plan B was the better choice.

REDEFINE THE OBJECTIVE AND OPTIONS

Now it's time to return to your original objective and update it. You may decide that your goal hasn't changed but your approach must be different. Or you may conclude that your goal was too aggressive and you need to phase in your change to build traction. Step one is having a really clear revised goal based on what you know now that you didn't know then—based on facts, not emotion.

Options can put things in perspective quickly. Have you ever thought you didn't like a choice, but when you compared it with the other options it started to look much better? The best example I have seen on the power of options came from the CEO of a Fortune 50 organization. She explained her rationale for some unpopular benefit changes to a very large group of employees, from new graduates to senior leaders. She spoke openly to the group as adults and never tried to spin or sell. She explained the business dilemma that prompted the change and told the group that the leadership team had researched and considered three viable options. She then shared the pros and cons of each before explaining the rationale for the final decision. She concluded that, after looking at the facts, the option chosen was the best one for employees. She took as many questions as needed to ensure the decision process was clear.

I watched the room transform in front of me as expressions softened and the mood lightened. Once all the options were clear and listeners understood the rationale, the group's perspective changed. In addition, the CEO built a lot of trust because she spoke openly and frankly about why she made her decision.

Options are very powerful because they remind us that we do have choices. Also, options are a great way to contrast and compare to make a better decision.

> **"Look at your options. There is never just one answer."**
> —*Tory Johnson*

As an example, Ellen wants to write professionally about her cause and passion. She has started blogging, but it hasn't caught on. There are a few people interested, but after two years her circle hasn't grown. She loves writing, but feels that to make it her career she needs more interest in her work. After much disappointment and advice from a trusted friend, she develops her options:

1. *Keep writing as she is today.* She loves writing and the number of people who read her work shouldn't matter, even though it will likely affect her ability to become a full-time writer.
2. *Change what she writes about.* Explore new topics and research what topics interest her core audience.
3. *Hire a marketing person.* Find an expert to help her reach new people.
4. *Engage more with others.* Connect with others more on social media and in her personal network. Contribute to others' ideas and successes,

identify guest blogging opportunities, and connect with like-minded groups, bringing her writing with her so she can share and learn from others.

5. *Stop writing.* It's frustrating that she can't build any momentum and change her career, so it may be best to pause for a while and try again later.

If Ellen's goal is to become a full-time writer, she has to choose the best option based on that goal. She finally concludes that it wasn't her writing holding her back; she needs to connect and engage more with others. She was standing back waiting for recognition and success. Her limited personal connections with others, especially in social media, meant that her share circle was too small and interest in her work wasn't growing. She decides to put her energy into option 4.

Options based on what's within your control can help you decide on a plan to best address what you learned in your mini-assessment.

WHAT'S YOUR PLAN B?

Now that you have looked at your options and what is in your control, it's time to create your plan. Based on what you learned, you may be thinking about changes in timing or a complete overhaul. Plan B isn't a failure, but a more educated attempt at your goal.

I felt one of my biggest work disappointments on a late flight home from New York. My team and I had presented important recommendations to the executive team on significant workforce changes that I felt were absolutely needed. The business case was sound and well researched. It was packaged in a compelling way and we'd held many pre-meetings to confirm we had the needed buy-in. We presented our recommendations confidently and persuasively—we thought. We even had visible support in the room, with many nodding heads. But there was one influential senior leader who'd had limited availability for preview discussions, yet her power and force could trump everyone else's. And that's exactly what happened.

As the meeting progressed, I thought we were confirming the support we needed. I even began to mentally prepare for questions on our next steps once we had the approval to continue. Our presentation represented almost a year of work, and I could see and feel the positive impact I knew this decision would have. Then, this influential senior leader stood up and in very angry and colorful language she boomed that this was not how we do things in this organization and she was adamantly opposed to it. Period. No discussion—she was out in a big way. It shut down the room and the project. Even though I felt sure that other leaders agreed with the recommendations, they were silent.

What I didn't know at the time was that her line in the sand actually built support with others on the executive team. They had bought into the change even though she hadn't. It took breaking the plan into two pieces and going at it again, but within a year the program happened with some minor tweaks. It was a significant change, and I don't think it would have happened without the pain of Plan A. But, Plan B eventually carried the day—just not on my timing.

Plan B needs a nice balance of optimism and reality. On one end of that spectrum you have some of our most amazing innovators, including Steve Jobs, Jeff Bezos, and Thomas Edison, who ignored the naysayers and moved forward. At the other end is the person who is overly responsive to feedback, changing the plan with every new conversation he has. Entrepreneurs can have more flexibility here than those inside more conservative or structured organizations, because the market casts the final vote. Find the balance for your work and situation.

Wave Maker Kathy Korman Frey, professor at The George Washington University and creator of the Hot Mommas® Project, a social venture designed to mentor women through case studies, shared the importance of focus when the interest began to dramatically increase:

> Word was getting out everywhere about the Hot Mommas® Project. We were in *Washington Post* magazine, NPR, *Wall Street Journal, Inc.* It was crazy. We were getting calls and interest from all over the world. Yet, we had problems. Surprisingly, our problems were associated with too much interest and too many requests. We were bombarded with ideas and things that people wanted us to do. We could bend to that and get involved in every single request, but we knew it would sink us. So, FOCUS became our new bumper sticker. We needed to focus on our core product and remember what we were here to do: Gather and share the stories of women for impact.

The important lesson in conducting your diagnostic and developing your options is to learn from setbacks and disappointments, even when the challenge comes because of success. Spend your energies on what is in your control. After you've had time to think and analyze, your Plan B will emerge and may very well be stronger than your first idea. Plan B may just be your best opportunity to realize your wave.

THINK TIME

You've gone through all of the steps of your diagnostic and you should have ideas on your Plan B. That is your goal—decide what's next.

1. What is your Plan B?
2. What will you do differently this time?
3. What is your step to get started?
4. Who else will be part of it with you?
5. What are the key milestones in your plan?

CHAPTER 10

Why Leaders Need More Wave Makers

Make Waves is built upon the idea that anyone can start a wave. Anyone. Most innovative and growing organizations need grassroots ideas, changes, and experimentation to realize their strategy. We also know that big changes in organizations eventually need sponsorship to become a reality. And leaders need new ideas and creative changes—including small ones—in order to reach their goals. Wonderful partnerships can evolve once there is recognition of this interdependency of goals.

Look at the business news today. *Innovation, change, creativity, disruption,* and *transformation*—these key words are in the headlines daily. Not as news, but to describe how organizations must adapt and evolve. Successful organizations don't stand still. They are evolving every day: it may be new markets, a new brand, a merger, new products, or a change to the way services are offered to the community. In this complex and changing world, leaders who head these organizations can't possibly know the answers to everything. It's just not possible. They need you.

They need you to start your wave if the organization is going to ultimately realize the new strategy. Successful changes have contributions from individuals who made an immeasurable impact because of their wave. Individuals like you who ask, "What can I do?" or "What if?"

Rich Sheridan has taken the importance of everyone's contribution to heart across the entire Menlo Innovations organization. Menlo Innovations disregards many of the standard business practices, such as a reliance on traditional hierarchy. The change to that flattened structure took commitment from everyone, not just a few top leaders. Menlo is built on paired working and high collaboration, with an empathetic approach in mind. High-Tech Anthropologists®, the name Menlo has for its user experience designers, have a lofty, self-stated goal: to end human suffering in the world as it relates to technology.

The team at Menlo Innovations has a fresh take on most aspects of running a business. As an example, Menlo's hiring process is called "Extreme Interviewing." It feels almost like speed dating. Applicants come to the office for a series of fast-paced interviews with several current employees. The employees look for what they call kindergarten skills, such as geniality, curiosity, and generosity. The Menlo view of Extreme Interviewing is that technical proficiency is less important than a candidate's "ability to make [his or her] partner look good."

After the interviews, the Menlonians who were involved gather to make some decisions. They argue, debate, and lobby one another. After a healthy debate, the interviewers vote with their thumbs based not on technical skills, but on kindergarten skills. What kind of collaboration did they see? Based on this evaluation, second interviews are granted to the applicants at the top of the list. In second interviews, candidates come in and work for a day, side by side with a Menlonian. Those who pass are invited for a three-week trial and are paid for their efforts. There isn't one leader who trumps everyone, nor do the most senior leader and the HR and Recruiting experts decide. The decision is completely made by other team members.

Like the team at Menlo Innovations, I believe that we are all leaders and contributors, even if most companies are not as progressive as Menlo in how these roles are applied. Some lead hundreds of people or an entire organization, while others lead themselves and the work they do each day. Regardless of where you sit, you play an important role in encouraging waves from your team, peers, and partners.

INNOVATION AND MAKING WAVES

As human beings, we are born with an interest in using our imagination and making the world better. Think back to kindergarten, when you were full of ideas, suggestions, and questions. Many of you remember your own questions, or have a child who regularly asks, "Why?" Why can't trains fly? What if we had birthday cakes for dogs? Why not? That creative mind-set gradually fades as we grow up, learn what's realistic, and apply the world's logic. And parental exhaustion has to be a factor too.

Many of us also slowly lose that zest for the unseen possibilities in our quest to show that we know the answer. Growing up and being part of bigger groups that we want to fit into also changes how we think. The desire for acceptance can overtake us.

By design, organizations in total will always be less innovative than many of the individuals who work there. Many businesses have grown because of scalable, efficient, and repeatable processes.

As stated on Bloomberg.com, in a January 2013 article, "The disciplines of management were invented, more than a hundred years ago, to drive variety out of organizations. The goal was to excise the irregularities, in an effort to ensure conformance to work rules, quality standards, timetables, and budgets."[1] Yet, the best ideas often come out of the irregularities, the new twist, or an idea that may not fit. This is where innovation begins, if we can keep the goal of efficiency in its proper place.

Companies like Cisco have taken steps to embed innovative thinking and practices throughout their business. They have created a framework for innovation by offering training, starting Innovation summits across the organization, organizing innovation leadership conferences, and recognizing those who innovate. Kate O'Keeffe, leader of the Services Innovation Excellence Center at Cisco, recently said, "Our model asserts that innovation cannot be the 'domain of the few' but must be the 'responsibility of the many.' "[2]

Everyone has a responsibility to innovate, create, and contribute. It is not the responsibility of top leadership or the executive team alone. It's not a feel-good move for engagement, either—though it's that too. Instead, innovation is an essential ingredient of realizing goals and growing a vital business.

BENEFITS OF WAVE MAKERS

Of course, not every situation calls for making waves. In organizations, repeatable processes and efficiency are essential to many parts of the business. And, as we have referenced throughout *Make Waves*, an idea is not a wave. It has to have purpose and real impact to the business, organization, community, or world. While organizations depend upon stability and repeatability to complete key processes effectively, they also need Wave Makers to create positive surges that move the group forward. Wave Makers are the ones who look for the better way, explore possibilities, see the new idea, and avoid the complacency of familiarity. Wave Makers serve as human catalysts for change and growth. You need them.

Wave Makers bring value because they:

- **Spark innovation.** As we discussed above, innovation comes from individuals with new and relevant ideas that will work. Every organization I know is looking for innovation, just in different ways and on different topics. Leaders can give inspiring presentations on the need to innovate and the importance for the organization's success. The hard part is connecting that philosophy to everyone who works there, not just the head of strategy or the chief innovation officer. Everyone has a role to play in innovation, and it takes individuals willing to step out, step up, and share their ideas.

    Wave Maker Lois Melbourne, co-creator and former CEO of Aquire, shared the connection between risk and innovation and creating a culture that encourages waves: "I think it's respect. You've got to respect people for taking the risk. You have to give them the ability to fail and not take a hit for their failures. Look at what worked and what didn't and learn from both. If an organization respects outside thought then anyone can say, 'Let's try this.' Encourage 'skunkworks,' risk taking, and exploration. Fear is anti-innovation."

> **"If someone tries something and it fails, then let it fail gracefully and not with fear."**
>
> —*Lois Melbourne*

- **Drive up performance.** It is amazing what two or three Wave Makers can do to raise the performance in a group or team. Most organizations have established performance measures to quantify success. If you are an entrepreneur, these measures are very real. They represent your paycheck as well as whether you can invest in that new employee. Performance is improved when everyone involved asks, "What can I do?" "Why? Is there a better way?" or "What if?"

  A few years ago, I saw the impact of a recent college graduate on a client team that had been doing their work the same way for years. She didn't judge or criticize, but she did start a change in that team without a big campaign to do so. She started using technology to streamline and improve access to meaningful data, made suggestions on work processes once she had a full understanding of the goals, and developed new techniques for packaging information. Her actions started to change the way the team worked, but she also raised the bar for the entire team's performance. And, she was smart in the way she did it. She kept her focus on the work, not judgment of those who did it.

- **Accelerate development.** Hands down, one of the best ways to accelerate your personal and professional development is working on a wave. Waves stretch us because we are taking on a challenge that hasn't been done before. There is no prescribed road map that tells you where to go. The experiences that I call on again and again for insights and learnings are the ones that were tied to some element of a change. Research tells us that we develop the most when in a stretch assignment or out of our comfort zone. Big changes create those opportunities.

  Wave Maker Jonathan Morris, chapter president in the Young Presidents' Organization, said that his wave changed him. He built relationships around the world, gained insights on how to collaborate and work together, and learned that traditional hierarchies can get in the way. He said that his wave made him a much better leader.

"I learned so much. There are benefits to being an agitator."
—*Jonathan Morris*

As we have discussed, waves extend beyond the boundaries of one job or role. They are aligned with bigger values that grow and build because of collaboration and interest in the change. Waves have patterns and flow and an evolving plan. And leaders advocate for growing the skills and capabilities of those in their organizations. It's important for you and the organization.

One of my clients has created a career plan that includes what they call "critical experiences." These are defined as experiences that accelerate an employee's development, increase capabilities, and, in turn, help the business. Changes can provide a critical experience across almost any type of work.

Alexis Sclamberg started a wave by founding Elevate GenY, a series of events for women in their twenties and thirties that focuses on integrating personal and professional development, health and wellness, and philanthropy. Alexis graduated from law school but was still searching for her ideal path. When she went to conferences she saw Generation Y's increasing demand for information, and it was a cause she cared about deeply.

Alexis explained:

Creating Elevate GenY has been a huge professional step for me. It is terrifying, sometimes overwhelming, and deeply gratifying all at the same time. From the moment my mom, Sharon Ufberg, and I dreamed up this big new venture, we knew without question we were going to go for it together. Having a trusted partner helps a lot. I have always heard that big rewards require big risks, and now I am personally living it. I am learning to trust my own intuition and be patient. Every day I feel proud of myself for committing to work hard for a vision that fulfills me.

Waves are ideal for career and capability acceleration.

- **Shake up the status quo.** If you or your leaders feel that the organization has gotten too stale or needs an influx of new ideas, then a Wave Maker can help. Is the status quo ready to be shaken? Entrepreneurs, by definition, shake up the status quo by redefining the market through a new and better product or service. Intrapreneurs can too.

Entire markets have been disrupted by a wave that eventually became a tsunami. Take the Blockbuster story. In 2011, Dish Network bought

Blockbuster's assets out of bankruptcy court for around $230 million. This is the same company that Viacom had previously paid $8.4 billion for and spun off into its own IPO. The fall was stunning in the market at the time. But if you had watched Blockbuster closely over the previous five to seven years, signs of its downfall were there among the omens of changes to come.

Reed Hastings started Netflix in 1998. He was a disappointed Blockbuster customer tired of the excessive late fees and thought there must be a better way. Blockbuster didn't take Netflix as a serious competitor at the time. In fact, two years later, Blockbuster could have bought Netflix for just $50 million, but showed no interest.

Six years after Netflix launched, Blockbuster finally realized it needed to enter the online DVD rental-by-mail space. By then, it was too late. Netflix was already turning a profit and Redbox had just launched.

There is no question that Blockbuster could have made countless decisions over a six-year period that may have turned the tide, but it didn't. I am sure that there were individuals inside Blockbuster who saw this coming. But, for whatever reason, their voices weren't heard or the status quo overtook them.

Leaders must be intentional up front. If they want more innovation, having the right people involved is essential. Finding Wave Makers is a core strategy to disrupt current thinking and conventional wisdom. And look at the opportunity that Reed Hastings created by experimenting with new subscription models at Netflix. It seems obvious now, but it wasn't then.

Any new change requires debate and discussion. Yet, the status quo is the only option that is usually not debated. It's the choice that becomes the "best" option without a decision ever being made. Every group needs individuals thinking about the next big thing, about how to make work better and improve our quality of life. You need people who aren't invested in the status quo.

ENCOURAGING WAVE MAKERS

Leaders signal the value of Wave Makers through their actions, such as welcoming new ideas, encouraging experimentation, and expecting leadership from everyone—not just those with the most senior titles. These small but important messages are sent every day. Do you have all of the answers or do you expect everyone to be a vital contributor? Let's look at the best strategies for how leaders can encourage Wave Makers.

Welcome New Ideas

New ideas are so essential in any change, but hierarchy and efficiency frequently get in the way. This is not just a feel-good move, it's essential for collaboration and innovation. I have been in many leadership conversations about a business challenge or a broken process that needed to change. You hope that executive-level meetings aren't the only place that conversation is happening. What do those closest to the work have to say? Some of the best ideas for change come from those actually doing the work.

We talked in chapter 5 about the power of the back-of-the-napkin conversation and not already having the answer when you show up. This is true whether you are leading a change or large organization. Encourage others who have the knowledge and capability to contribute.

Even basic habits, such as asking "what do you think?", including diverse perspectives, and actively engaging those closest to the work demonstrate that new ideas aren't only expected, but valued.

I've seen some companies do this formally to ensure that ideas are part of a structured innovation or change planning process. But it can be done informally too. One of the best informal examples I've seen came from the CEO of a smaller organization with off-the-charts growth. Every week he's in town, he takes a couple of hours to walk the building and talk to everyone. He listens and asks questions about their work. He takes ideas on how to improve. By setting a tone of openness to input and ideas, he increases the likelihood that when someone has a breakthrough idea, he will hear about it.

Leaders must also set expectations for the timing of new ideas. There are times when new ideas have to pause because you are implementing the ideas you decided upon last month. Unless there is a business reason that says the implementation won't work or needs to be revisited, save it until the next version or upgrade. Melisa Miller's organization, at Alliance Data Retail Services, focused on contributing ideas where they were needed, but didn't ask for ideas on the key business outcomes, which were already established. This balance of value and timing is best shared openly.

Likewise, we are most effective when we qualify our ideas before we begin sharing. You have probably seen the person who has great ideas but is an idea factory. Rather than influencing others, he shares any and all ideas with others without prequalification for value, relevance, or alignment with goals.

I spoke to a friend recently about my book, and this topic came up. She mentioned someone on her team who had great ideas with a ratio of about 1:10—one great idea for every ten shared. If you stayed with him, you'd eventually hear a few great ideas, but it would take a lot of time and patience—time and patience that most aren't willing to give. My friend advised him that ideas have to be more than just the top-of-mind thoughts. They need some internal prequalification for impact and relevance before they can be successfully shared. Create the opportunity for hearing new ideas and also keep your ideas relevant and impactful.

Encourage Experimentation

To encourage means to support, hope for, and enable. As I shared in chapter 6, experimentation is testing under controlled conditions and trying a new approach to gain experience and knowledge. What happens when we experiment? Some things work and some don't. Our hypothesis is tested. Experiments provide information we didn't know before. So, "encourage experimentation" can be another way to say we support that which may not work. Are you ready for that statement?

Some leaders say that they encourage experimentation, yet there is no tolerance when something goes wrong. I distinguish between an experiment that didn't work and a mistake made because a process wasn't followed or someone didn't address a customer problem. The latter is very different from deliberate experimentation, which naturally includes problems and mistakes. Expect them.

Experiments are, by design, controlled. They are designed to answer certain questions and test assumptions. I'm not a fan of associating the word "failure" with experiments. Yes, scientifically, some experiments fail to prove the hypothesis. But, unless it's an all-or-nothing proposition, failure is part of learning what will work.

Be Willing to Sit in the Back

Be willing to let others lead the experiment or test the new idea. Leaders often believe that having all of the answers is a key ingredient for respect and success. And, as a business community and society, we regularly reinforce that belief by our admiration of the all-knowing and the individualist. Yet we know that inviting others to be part of starting and creating a change is essential for innovation and a sustainable wave. Leaders must be willing to step to the sidelines and let others be visible, make important decisions, and be in the front of the room. These actions promote shared leadership and the emphasis on 'what's in it for us'.

One of the most impressive executives I worked for was masterful at being in charge when needed, but also being part of the team so that others could lead too. He encouraged those with great ideas to share and test them and gave them some limited funding or support. These simple acts showed how much he valued new ideas and the input of others.

I'm not recommending an abdication of leadership, and there are many situations that call for a leader to stand in front and take charge. Yet, if your goal is to encourage broad participation and incorporate new ideas, you have to share the stage. And if you work in a community effort, this is absolutely essential, as volunteers have complete choice in how they spend their time.

We also know that open participation supports engagement and commitment, both essential ingredients in building a community around your wave. So, there are many benefits. And this philosophy has been a key principle of revered leaders, such as Nelson Mandela.

Richard Stengel, editor of *Time* magazine, spent years interviewing Nelson Mandela and collaborated with him on his autobiography, *Long Walk to Freedom*. In an interview with Voice of America, Stengel said, "Lead from the front is the more conventional kind of leading that we know—getting up on the podium and giving a speech or saying follow me. But leading from the back is a different idea."[3]

Nelson Mandela embodied this idea of leading from behind. He provided the example and the values and let others lead in their own way with his gentle guidance.

Listen Well

We've talked about listening throughout *Make Waves*. It's important always and it's especially important when the goal is to encourage Wave Makers. The absolute first step in engaging with someone who wants to start a change is listening. Most of the Wave Makers I interviewed started with, "I have an idea. What do you think?" Just imagine the reaction if the other person was busy checking her phone or said, "Maybe later, I'm in a hurry."

We are a very distracted society right now. The competition for our attention is fierce, and our attention span is getting shorter. As a result, listening is becoming a lost art. Now, when I meet someone who is a full body listener, it is memorable. I believe that one of our greatest gifts is listening to someone so that they feel heard. I am working on this constantly. Not thinking of the next question, not anticipating my answer, not assessing, and not thinking of something else or doing something else.

This is probably the simplest yet most valued way of encouraging others to start or be part of the change. Just the act of really listening takes you out of the leader mode and into an attitude of "We are in this together."

Recognize and Reward Wave Making

Changes aren't your standard project or initiative. There will inevitably be bumps and ongoing adjustments. There may not be immediate success, as most changes take time, so persistence and setting aside the ego are essential. This is not the conventional wisdom on how to fast-track a career. But, it can be the right way. In fact, many of the Wave Makers felt that starting their change had a transformative effect on their personal growth and success.

Bruce Ballengee started Pariveda Solutions because he wanted to create a very different organization, including how contribution is recognized and rewarded. Bruce recalled the early discussions of starting the business: "We'll do consulting, but it has to be interesting. We want to think about our industry differently—with a new business model. Our model will be almost inverted from the traditional business model. On the surface they don't look that different. But you get underneath the covers and it's really different, and that's what makes it interesting and very challenging at multiple levels."

Bruce believes in providing a more balanced and transparent reward structure with senior leaders and the rest of the organization so that financial success is attainable by more than just a very few at the top.

Leaders can enable changes with more than just encouragement. The real proof comes when executives recognize those who step out. Consider:

- Do you subtly penalize those who led an experiment that didn't work?
- Do you brand those with new ideas as too ambitious or as not knowing their place?
- Do you rely on hierarchy and wonder why an analyst shared her ideas rather than letting her director be the one to speak up?
- Do you withhold a promotion or salary increase for those who achieved success in nontraditional ways?

If you don't formally reward and recognize those who start and make changes, it won't matter what you say because what you do doesn't match up. A few years ago a new client called me because their engagement program wasn't working as they had hoped. After research and interviews with employees, we discovered that their stated strategy and vision for collaboration and an involved workforce hadn't been translated to operational decisions. This company promoted those who didn't demonstrate these behaviors and gave the greatest salary increases to some who left a wake of employee problems in their path. Their operational decisions and actions were out of alignment with their vision. In the real world, actions always trump words.

DEVELOPING WAVE MAKERS

Wave Makers don't just appear. Some have a natural instinct to think creatively, be bold, or see the unseen. That insight can be developed with the right experiences and environment. Let's look at ideas for how to develop the capability in others to become a Wave Maker.

Bruce Ballengee, Wave Maker and CEO of Pariveda Solutions, said that he views his purpose and that of the organization as teaching and developing. He is a big advocate of active mentoring, which he says is one of the things he enjoys most about his work. Bruce said, "The best part of my work is developing talented people from the time they join after college to when they reach their potential in this organization. Pariveda is really a platform to teach and help others learn. I have a lot of fun teaching other people, including a very early exposure to networking for life—the idea of growing relationships and helping others—paying it forward."

> "Encouragement is lost in the world today."
> —*Julie Porter*

Ask Questions That Teach

We know that waves are often developed not because one person was a creative genius, but because of asking insightful questions. These questioners have a habit of exploring and being curious about why and how. As a leader, you can develop others to start changes by asking them questions and teaching them to eventually ask the same questions of themselves.

Earlier in my career, I worked for a wise leader, Don Monaco, who typically responded to recommendations with, "Walk me through your thinking," "What alternatives did you consider?" "Why did you choose this option?" "What outcomes can we expect if we do this?" and "What will it cost?" His questions taught me a lot about developing recommendations and the thought process that needed to take place before I came forward with new options and ideas. He engrained this way of thinking into his team, so that we learned to ask ourselves these questions. And you can too, even if your leaders don't ask.

Give White Space Assignments

White space is my way of saying the work is not fully defined or more clarity is needed. These are the times when there is no precedent or clear road map. A design is needed. The objective or value is defined, but that is all. And the exact outcome may not even be known yet—just the problem.

It's up to the individuals involved to create what doesn't exist today using research, insights, and instinct. Of course, waves meet that criteria, but so does a new role that didn't exist before, a position in a newly formed company or environment, or a dramatic change that renders the old rules obsolete. One of my "go-to" questions when I want to understand the ability of an individual to design and create is, "How effective is he with a blank piece of paper?" It's another way of asking if that person can thrive in the "white space"—the undefined and the unseen with no road map.

> "On a wave, you have to invent the rules."
> —*Charley Johnson*

At Accenture, I had the opportunity to work on acquisitions or consolidations in new markets and businesses. Even though I was in a well-established consulting firm, some of my projects made me feel like I was working at a start-up, because we created completely new strategies, culture, plans, and processes for these new businesses. These experiences are what we joked at the time were "career dog years"— when you gain seven years of experience all rolled into one because everything was new and hard. Even so, these experiences were a true difference maker for me.

Leaders can plan these assignments to build Wave Maker capability. And we can each look for these types of assignments to develop our capability as well. This experience in the white space helps everyone who can handle it.

Put People out of Their Zone

We all have these zones that fit our expertise, where we are most comfortable and confident. Have you ever noticed that when an outsider comes in he often has an observation or insight that those working there for months missed? It is because someone with a fresh perspective can see what others can't. It's not that he is wiser; he just doesn't have the blinders that come after looking at something too long.

In writing this book, I have asked friends and colleagues to read and give me their thoughts. I recently told a friend, "I've looked at this so long sometimes I can't see it anymore." Have you noticed that we see how others can solve their problems much more easily than we can solve our own?

You can develop future Wave Makers by proactively looking for stretch roles and assignments. It's not setting someone up to fail, but asking her to take on a new role, opportunity, or project that is one step beyond the comfort zone. This experience helps your people expand their horizons and see the world in a new way. And, it develops a confidence in stretching—especially with the right support.

While there was no one telling me to start my business, I decided to jump in. It was out of my zone at first and I felt some anxiety as a result. While the work content was familiar, the way in which it was delivered, as well as all the tasks and responsibilities that come with starting a new business, were completely new. I had come from a very large organization with tools, support, and access to almost anything. I laugh now as I look back on some of my naïve beliefs and assumptions at the beginning. The experience of starting my business was a process of developing both my strengths and my weaknesses, and it changed my perspective on more issues than I can count.

Promote Thinking Wider

In bigger organizations, it's easy to slip into roles and teams that are isolated from others and start to define success very narrowly. Silos are one of the most common business problems in general, and especially if there is a priority on innovation and collaboration. Leaders need organizational groups to deliver on their promises and commitments, but not when the group becomes more important than the larger goal.

Asking individuals to lead a project that is broader than their role and function naturally expands thinking. It also develops an understanding of the needs in other organizational groups through firsthand exposure and experience. It's a great way to gain perspective and see the business and the market more holistically.

Share How to Start a Change

My main goal in writing *Make Waves* is to provide ideas and insights for those who want to start a wave. There are strategies, habits, and actions that will increase the chance of your wave building momentum and success. While some use these strategies naturally and by instinct, I believe they can absolutely be learned.

There are Wave Makers all around us. Some work in big organizations and others in small ones. Others are entrepreneurs. Some are in their twenties and others are in their sixties. Some start big-scale changes and others start with a pebble that will make lasting ripples and turn into something bigger. In my research, even with all of their differences, there were patterns and similarities because all were starting a change. The pattern tells us there is something there to learn. Starting a change isn't random or an innate quality you had at birth.

If you educate yourself and develop the skills needed to start and sustain a change, the likelihood of being able to repeat it increases dramatically. You probably have people who meet this profile in your organization today. You don't call them Wave Makers today, but you know who they are. As I said in chapter 1, when I asked trusted friends and colleagues for their Wave Makers, they all quickly understood and shared their examples. Make sure that those who have made waves in your organization share and help build that capability in others. And recognize them!

LEADERS AND WAVE SPONSORSHIP

If you start a bigger wave inside an organization, at some point you will need sponsorship. Strategically identify those who are in a position to sponsor or connect. If your change needs a sponsor in your organization, zero in on exactly what you need first and then determine those who can best help you. You may need funding, expertise, or someone who can influence others. Sponsorship is always important, but it's essential to know the kind of sponsorship you need.

Likewise, if you are a sponsor for a Wave Maker, determine how you can best offer your support. Here are a few types of sponsors that Wave Makers may need:

Advocate. The Advocate is behind you and the effort and will tell anyone about the importance of your change. He is in your corner privately and publicly. Advocates usually see your change as aligned with a broader vision or strategy they support, either personally or organizationally.

Connector. The Connector is a role leaders can play inside or outside of the organization. When I started my business, I had many Connectors who said, "You should know..." and they made that introduction happen. Also, leaders can be champions for grassroots efforts inside their organization and connect Wave Makers to other sponsors who can help.

Validator. The Validator is the expert who confirms that your idea is sound and that you have considered all of the relevant issues. The Validator can add credibility to your idea or change by giving it a stamp of approval, even if she isn't actively involved.

Funder. The Funder provides the money you need to get started, experiment, or engage others. Inside an organization, it is the person who controls the budget. If you are an entrepreneur, it may be an investor who funds your idea or new business. A Connector may help you find the right Funder or a valued funding source. Of course, as we discussed earlier, there are also crowd funding options for entrepreneurs as well.

Advisor. The Advisor may not be a visible supporter, but he provides wise guidance and mentoring as needed. The Advisor is a sponsor who has typically accomplished a relevant goal and is well qualified to help you strategize and consider options. Sometimes Advisors may be other types of sponsors as well, though not always. I have had many Advisors in my career who offered valued wisdom and counsel even when not visibly involved in the work.

If you are a leader in a position to be a sponsor, it's important to ask Wave Makers, "What role can I play? How can I help you?" It takes this type of advocacy from leaders to power grassroots efforts and experiments. Likewise, if you want to start a wave, identify the kinds of sponsors that you need.

Kristi Erickson, a PeopleResults colleague and former Accenture partner, and I were recently preparing for a leadership conference. We were discussing how leaders can play a role in activating waves throughout their organizations. We decided that a leader can really be a "human Kickstarter." Be the one who helps waves build momentum and supports new ideas, a go-to Advisor and Connector. Help a Wave Maker get the financial support he needs. Kristi gave two examples of waves that originally began within her team. She saw her role as helping these Wave Makers connect to the right people and find funding, and she influenced other leaders who were needed as key sponsors. She wore multiple sponsor hats to make it happen.

Leaders everywhere can decide to be difference makers and help needed changes see the light of day. Determine the sponsors you need to make your wave happen, then work to get them involved.

THINK TIME

1. How can you as a Wave Maker, or as a leader of Wave Makers, connect making waves to innovation in your group?
2. What can Wave Makers do to make your organization or community better?
3. What actions can you take to encourage Wave Makers on your team or within your organization?
4. What actions can you take for yourself and for your team to develop the skills and knowledge needed to be a Wave Maker?
5. What kind of sponsors do you need to realize your wave? Who can play this role for you?
6. What kind of sponsor can you be for others as they pursue their changes and goals?

PART 4

Inspiration

Meet the Wave Makers

This is my chance to introduce all of the Wave Makers that I have featured throughout the book. All were "nominated" by at least one trusted colleague because of admiration for how they started their wave. After receiving many recommendations and considering my own, I selected this diverse group to study and research in more detail. I added their stories to my experiences and to conversations with countless others not featured in the book.

This chapter shares who they are, their wave, why they are inspiring, and one of their many memorable comments. Their stories are woven throughout the book so that you can learn what they did and why they did it, in the hope that their experiences will be instructive for your wave.

I don't want to give the impression that these Wave Makers are perfect or superhuman. They would all quickly tell you that they aren't and that their changes weren't perfect. And each one reminded me several times in our discussions that they didn't make their change happen alone. Yet, they all went to the core questions I have shared throughout *Make Waves* of "What can I do?", "How can I make a difference?", and "What if?"

At first glance, you may think, "What does this group have in common?" After all, these Wave Makers include a high school student, the manager of a Major League Baseball team, entrepreneurs, senior executives in the Fortune 500, a #1 *New York Times* best-selling author, community leaders, and millennials in the first phase of their careers. Yet, when I studied how they realized their changes, common themes and patterns emerged. I believe that we can learn from them and from the other stories in this book, even if their situations and careers are quite different than ours.

Honestly, my interviews with these Wave Makers were my favorite part of writing this book. I have spent much of my career involved in organizational change, but these interviews felt so different to me. I found it fascinating to look at a change differently—through the eyes, decisions, and actions of one pivotal person.

As we talked, I asked each of them to picture you, the reader, sitting close by listening in on our conversation to learn more. This chapter is from them to you.

I wrote this book with the goal of inspiring others to act and start a wave, yet each of these Wave Makers ended up inspiring me.

Let me introduce you.

BRUCE BALLENGEE

Bruce's Wave

Bruce had already had a successful career in technology consulting when he created Pariveda Solutions in 2003. From the start, his vision was that this organization would be different. He wanted to provide the opportunity for rapid advancement, place a priority on relationships, and ensure that financial rewards are more evenly distributed, not confined to top leadership. Bruce shared with pride that new college graduates have the opportunity to progress to vice president in ten years.

He and his team have also turned the idea of traditional networking on its head. Bruce believes that everyone who works for Pariveda is in sales, represents the brand everywhere they go, and that networking is a way of life, not an extracurricular. The company considers individual networking metrics and relationship building as a part of individual contribution.

Bruce said, "Pariveda is really a platform for us to teach and develop complete and effective IT executives. That requires an understanding of sales and the market, and how to build relationships." Pariveda Solutions's rapid growth and retention of key talent has encouraged the wave to continue.

Bruce Is Inspiring Because . . .

Bruce relied on unconventional and creative ideas, even when they ran counter to the latest trends. He and his team developed an organization to benefit not just the top leaders but everyone who works there. He also has a very different view of networking and reminded me that business is ultimately about relationships—relationships that help get things done, collaborate for the client, and grow your business.

And, I find the people I know at Pariveda Solutions live by their philosophy of generosity to others without an expectation of something in return. It's embedded in their culture.

Advice for Other Wave Makers

- Trust your passion, not your ego. Passion will see you through and you'll have to fall back on that at times. Let your passion be your guide and point you toward true north.
- It will be difficult, fraught with problems and risk. If it doesn't work out, it's okay. You still did the right thing. You've fulfilled a large part of your potential by doing that. You get more than one chance. And if you do succeed, then you just say, "Well, that's fantastic!"

> "You have to give gifts all along the way. It's about giving gifts—gifts of your time, your ideas, sometimes of your money, but mostly your time and your thoughts. And, your empathy. These are the biggest gifts you can give. Over time you'll earn much of that in return, but that's not why you do it."

MARK BENTON

Mark's Wave

Mark is a senior director at PepsiCo. His wave was leading the design and implementation of a talent management and learning strategy within the company's Research and Development (R&D) organization. Mark began by building a global network of associates to learn what was working across the organization and to share his plans. He partnered with countless business leaders to design a new global R&D virtual university that relied on the expertise of business leaders. He created a new career model while using the best ideas from around the world to make it happen. He worked with R&D leadership to create the company's first Global R&D Fellows program based on developing and recognizing the most distinguished R&D thought leaders within PepsiCo. Mark has led a global change through involvement with hundreds of stakeholders and thousands of R&D professionals, enabling employees to grow their careers and capability in new ways.

His strategy was to move quickly, use what's working, and build on that to jumpstart the effort. Experiment and try new ideas. Involve many and listen. He created a global network of advisors who rolled up their sleeves. Then, as new changes were introduced, he used technology to enable it, but he and his team also got out of their offices because they knew that some changes require an in-person presence. This is a multiyear change effort that has evolved and grown over time. Mark said that it is bigger now than what he envisioned when he started, because he and his team adapted and developed new ideas as progress was made.

Mark Is Inspiring Because . . .

Mark is inspiring because of the way he used his influence and partnering skills to reach his goals when there were many diverse ideas and opinions to be considered.

Mark also mastered experimentation and testing by trying new ideas, as well as taking successes in one part of the business and trying them in another. He found a way to begin and move while also designing, a process he described as ' "flying the plane while we were still building it." Also, his tremendous respect for others has built trusted relationships throughout his team and across the business. He is a role model of a values-based leader.

Advice for Other Wave Makers

- Have a clear vision, even if you change it over time.
- Get others involved in your change and vision. Most people vastly underestimate how much time and work getting folks brought into the change really takes.
- Work with integrity so that you don't realize your wave at the expense of others. I feel great about a change when I see everybody getting to the new place together.
- Listen to others. Treat everyone with respect even if you disagree.

"Anyone trying to move a change forward is going to have resistance. Don't squash resistance. Use that knowledge as power. I always try to be open to feedback and listen. I think fully understanding your resistance is powerful. Then, you know what you are facing."

ERIC BUHRFEIND

Eric's Wave

Eric Buhrfeind, a former Accenture Partner, saw a need to better attract and retain the best recruits in emerging global markets, particularly in India. At the time, candidates in India had almost unlimited options as more companies established a presence there. Eric took on the challenge even though it wasn't his sole responsibility to solve. Eric said, "I started thinking 'How can we take our world-class training and make it more attractive in these markets?'"

He played to Accenture's strength and developed a plan to partner with a world-class academic institution to launch a prestigious certification program. He relied heavily on leadership from his team, especially Allison Horn and Paul Richardson. No one was asking for this certification, yet Eric requested a budget to test ideas when budgets were tight. He had no ROI analysis to back up his recommendation, just a few indicators that it would fit the need. He persisted and received some seed money to experiment on a small scale. This initial experimentation created interest, and it ultimately led to a strategic partnership with MIT that elevated Accenture's brand in these markets. It significantly enhanced recruiting and retention results.

The program was highly valued by employees in all markets. Accenture won awards and was recognized externally for this partnership, and it became a differentiator with clients. This program has accelerated, endured and sustained since its inception almost ten years ago. It all started by Eric asking 'what can I do?' and kicking around ideas in the back of a cab.

Eric Is Inspiring Because . . .

Eric took on a challenge because of an essential business need. He developed an idea that had never been done before and that he knew would require a lot of influence to pull off. In a large and global organization like Accenture, he had to influence and involve many just to get the budget to experiment. He then spoke to hundreds of people about his wave, often one on one, and built a community of support. And his persistence paid off. It worked.

Advice for Other Wave Makers

- Make sure you have both a great idea and a need. You need both.
- Have a good concept to test first.
- You need *both* passion and substance. You can't have one without the other.
- Be organized even though you must adjust as you go.
- Gain alignment of your vision with leadership and establish a coalition to bring it to life
- It will happen by talking to people one by one, step by step.

"I had a leader say to me, 'Eric, why are you doing this? You're asking us to spend money at a tough time. Our clients aren't asking for this. We're not asking you to do this, and our people aren't asking for this.' And, that was a tough question. I responded that this will be a game changer for us and I don't think anyone else can do it. There will be ROI, but I can't tell you what it will be yet—but, it will be significant. I ask you to trust me. I'm only requesting a small amount of money to experiment, hold focus groups and see what this can become. I got the approval for this baby step. It got us started."

FIONA GRANT

Fiona's Wave

Fiona was behind the introduction of domestic partner benefits at Accenture, even though overseeing employee benefits wasn't part of her formal job responsibilities. Fiona was the first to tell me that she didn't do this alone. But she played a vital role in finding a way to make this policy change a reality. She began by working with a small group of leaders who also believed in offering this benefit.

For Fiona and those she recruited, this wave represented the intersection of a proclamation by the CEO with a personal event. Then-CEO of Accenture Joe Forehand announced that he wanted to usher in a period of bold change. A key competitor had just announced plans to offer domestic partner benefits. Those two events signaled that there was a readiness to consider the move at Accenture.

Fiona knew that the business case and rationale had to be fact based and unemotional, given the organization and the topic. She wanted to outline a very clear return on investment. She also knew that education was required because she learned that there were misconceptions about the policy. Besides working with a core team who believed in making the change, she involved other trusted leaders, who reviewed material and provided input. This helped build early sponsorship from some of the most respected leaders at that time.

On the personal front, Fiona and her partner had decided to have a child, whom they named Daisy. She soon realized that she had no way to cover them both on her insurance at work. Her personal situation not only motivated her, but helped others see the real need. It translated the policy discussion to a real-life situation they understood. It was the best education she could have provided. She found that other parents had empathy for her, and Daisy's imminent arrival made the need very real.

Fiona used facts and took special care to build support for her recommendation. Also, the confidence others had in her, and in the rest of the team, was an essential ingredient in realizing her goal.

Fiona Is Inspiring Because...

Fiona's story intrigued me from the beginning because I knew Accenture well and that no major decisions were made without research and thoughtful consideration. I wondered how she was able to build interest and momentum behind her idea. I found her inspiring because she humanized her wave, yet she also let the facts guide her work.

Also, Fiona's openness and transparency were inspiring. She had an inner confidence in her views while also demonstrating respect for those she hoped to educate. She had such enthusiasm, humor, and honesty that she was the perfect champion for making this change in a global management consulting, technology and outsourcing company.

Advice for Other Wave Makers

- Definitely have a little core group. If you were by yourself, that would be spectacularly hard.
- Be clear without being overly passionate. Share your ideas and recommendations as simply as possible—break them down into the executive summary version.
- Use the decision maker's own words and phrases in your request. It will be harder to resist!
- You don't get what you don't ask for. But you don't have to ask for the world. Be an incrementalist. You can always go back for more.

"Our business case was so strong, there was no way they could say no to it. We'd sorted everything out already—competitor view, return on investment, actual cost, likely concerns, and benefits. We thought of everything and got lots of input. We knew that was what it would take."

CLINT HURDLE

Clint's Wave

Clint Hurdle is known for changing the culture of clubhouses player by player. When Clint first joined the Pittsburgh Pirates, he listened because he wanted to learn more about each member of the team. He said a player has to trust you before you can coach him. Clint said, "He needs to trust that he is more than just a lefthander with speed, but a human being. And trust that you have his best interest at heart."

He then talks to players about how they think, as he believes success begins inside our heads. He encourages always thinking positively, focusing on what's in your control, and believing in yourself. His goal is to give three encouragements for one correction. But he also said another part of trust is being honest and telling the truth. Clint believes that some healthy conflict and sharing different points of view are essential. He said this is how we understand and build trust with one another, which is needed for any change.

Clint translates this openness and transparency into how the club communicates with one another. He often uses an exercise called three up, three down. Everyone shares three things working well and three things that aren't. Everyone participates even if there is discomfort at first. Eventually, the issues are out in the open and the team learns from the conversation. Over time, the exercise becomes less significant because there is a common understanding and everything is out in the open.

Clint's ability to change the culture has translated into success on the field, including winning the National League pennant with the Colorado Rockies in 2007; in 2013, he led the Pittsburgh Pirates to their first playoff berth since 1992. Clint was named National League Manager of the Year in 2013.

Clint Is Inspiring Because . . .

Clint is inspiring because of his faith and that he knows what matters, even in a high-expectations business like Major League Baseball. He is dedicated to influencing how players think and the importance of staying positive not only with others, but within themselves. He sends out a daily thoughts and affirmations to his e-mail list of over a thousand friends, players, players' wives, and other coaches. We get a daily reminder of his outlook on life that always ends with, "Make a difference today. Love, Clint." Clint is making a difference and he encourages others, like me, to pause and remember to do the same.

Advice for Other Wave Makers

- It takes courage to have patience. It's important because change takes time.
- Be more comfortable with your internal thermostat than the external thermostat.
- You need intent, conviction, and execution. You can't start a change without all three.
- You develop trust with complete transparency. You have nothing to lose, nothing to hide.

> "You never start by talking about the results you want on the field. It's about how the players talk and think. They need to take ownership of the game and of the team. When that happens, the results will take care of themselves."

BRETT HURT

Brett's Wave

Brett is a repeat entrepreneur who has been pioneering e-commerce innovations since 1998 and online communities since 1982. As co-founder of Bazaarvoice, Brett served as CEO from its inception in 2005 until November 2012, during which time he led the company through its IPO, a follow-on offering, and two acquisitions.

Previously, Brett founded Coremetrics, in February 1999, after spending ten years developing Internet-based software. He helped grow Coremetrics into a leading marketing analytics solution for the e-commerce industry. Prior to Coremetrics, Brett was the founder and CEO of Hurt Technology Consulting and BodyMatrix, an online retailer of sports nutrition products.

Brett, like many Wave Makers, has had numerous waves, but his passion for open access and sharing led to the creation of Bazaarvoice. He believes that encouraging customers to comment openly on products online simply mirrors the human affinity for sharing our views with one another.

Brett Is Inspiring Because . . .

Brett inspired me because of his ability to see the unseen. He also embodies the principle that movement creates movement and momentum creates momentum. I was impressed that, on his first full day of working on the creation of Bazaarvoice, he was already selling the concept to future customers. He didn't wait for the formal marketing materials, the office setup, or the perfect website. He has a bias for action and got started.

As Brett said, "I always recommend two books to entrepreneurs, *The Bootstrapper's Bible*, by Seth Godin, and *The Art of the Start* by Guy Kawasaki. Both are about jumping in and getting started. Engineers often want to build a product, launch it, and then sell it. It doesn't work that way. I've seen a lot of people build products that no one cares about, waste millions of dollars and years of their life—because they're afraid to talk with the customer.

Advice for Other Wave Makers

- If you have a dream, you have to get moving or it's never going to happen. You've got to get going.
- Surround yourself with other people who are incredibly passionate about your cause.
- If you just keep putting yourself out there over and over and over again, and you authentically believe in what you're doing, eventually you're going to change the world. It's that simple.
- I am a believer in God. I am a believer that the universe conspires to make you successful. That doesn't necessarily mean financially successful. There are lots and lots of incredible people at nonprofits who haven't had much financial success but have completely transformed the world. Gandhi never had financial success but he changed the world. But, they didn't do it by sitting on their butt. They did it by starting.

"There are a lot of people, unfortunately, who either haven't found their authentic dream, or they know what it is and they're too afraid to go after it. Or, they don't know how to get moving. To those people I say, get a mentor, read some books. Get started now."

CHARLEY JOHNSON

Charley's Wave

Charley Johnson formerly owned a manufacturing company, and he left his company, career, and significant success, as the world defines it, behind. He said for the first time he looked forward to the weekends and he no longer had the motivation to motivate himself, much less others. He saw the movie *Pay It Forward* in 2000 and it inspired him. He got involved and started doing many side projects to encourage the Pay it Forward movement. Then, in 2011, he became fully committed to the growth of Pay it Forward. He said, "As much as I love security and don't like to change, I wanted to make sure I did something. Are you going to back up all those quotes you talked about doing something important, all those times you watched some athlete do something at the very last second after all the hard work? Are you bold enough to step out and actually try to do something that could change people's lives?"

Charley then set in motion the connection of a global network of Pay it Forward groups dedicated to making the world a better place. Now head of the Global Pay it Forward Movement and president of the Pay it Forward Foundation, he created many ways for people around the world to get involved. They introduced the Pay it Forward bracelet, a physical reminder to do good that has been sent to more than two million people in 125 countries, the "PIF Experience," the Pay it Forward Movement site, as well as a "Pay it Forward Hall of Fame," with Catherine Ryan Hyde, author of the novel *Pay It Forward*, as the first inductee.

Charley Is Inspiring Because...

Charley was motivated solely by doing work that matters and, as he said, "when he's sixty that he'll know he's done it." He was completely transparent and open with me about his goals, as well as the fears he faced to get there. He said he likes security and doesn't like change, yet he left his own lucrative career behind to engage thousands of others in the Pay it Forward cause. He had fears, but he did it anyway. I also found that Charley modeled looking for *your* answer, not the *right* answer.

Advice for Other Wave Makers

- Do what you think is right.
- There's no silver bullet. There's no book out there that's going to give you the answers. There's no individual out there who can give you all the answers, or can make what you want happen. Learn as much as you can, but it will come down to you deciding what to do.
- You need to choose to do it first, and then find the way to get it done.
- Be ready to fail. Not everything you do is going to work.

> "We're a very gullible group. Some famous guy or woman at the top of a company writes a book. They're writing what they believe, from their perspective, and their own opinion about what worked for them. But, there's no way it's going to work like that for everybody. Probably one of the biggest problems is that a lot of people fail because they think that they have to do these specific things that some big name did, and it's just not the way it is anymore. Their situation was different."

TORY JOHNSON

Tory's Wave

Tory has had several waves, all based on her dedication to helping entrepreneurs and women get what they want out of life. Her journey began early in her career when she was unexpectedly fired from a job she loved. That permanent scar started Tory's first shift from employee to entrepreneur. She started by helping other women grow careers through her first business, *Women for Hire*. She then expanded into enabling entrepreneurs to create their dream businesses built on their passion (spark) and getting out there and making it happen (hustle). She created *Spark and Hustle,* which provides entrepreneurs the tools, ideas, a book, events, and a vital network to start and grow their businesses. Tory's latest wave is *The Shift,* based on her #1 *New York Times* best-selling book that inspires women to take control of their weight and their health. Tory is a weekly contributor on *Good Morning America*, a contributing editor to *SUCCESS* magazine, and a keynote speaker on getting what you want out of life.

Tory has not only helped many women and entrepreneurs create their dream, she has enabled a vital community around her. Her conferences and events are certainly part of her business, but this organic community helps one another by cross-promoting, sharing, and giving each other advice. Tory is also very generous with her wisdom and shares it openly, which is one of the reasons her circle continues to grow.

Tory Is Inspiring Because . . .

Tory is one of the most accountable people I have ever met. She lives in the mindset, discussed throughout *Make Waves,* of "What can I do?" If you spend much time with Tory, you learn that excuses and feeling sorry for yourself won't work.

Spend your energy on what you can do and if you hit a wall, find your Plan B. What's next? Keep going.

Tory has built her business by helping others do the same. She is inspiring because she shares her wisdom along with practical advice. I've heard many stories of her taking the time to offer guidance or encouragement that made all the difference to a new entrepreneur. And that open, sharing mind-set has been a key ingredient in creating a community that learns from her and from one another.

Advice to Other Wave Makers

- *Know* what you want to do. *Do* what you want to do.
- Know the big "WHY." When you're super clear on your WHY, nothing derails you because you're so committed to WHY you want to do this. You're going to put in the time and the effort. You're going to see it through. When your WHY is so strong, it's a lot harder to give up when things don't happen on the ideal timetable.
- Do you have the time to commit to this? Things don't happen overnight. I think one of the biggest obstacles is that people abandon ship too soon. Ideas are a dime a dozen. It's all about the execution. Realize it's going to take some time. When you recognize that from the outset, it's easier to adjust your expectations. You can be impatient—that's okay—but don't let that be a reason to give up too soon.

> "The biggest obstacles I see are our self-imposed obstacles. I want to help people get out of their own way and recognize that they can do it."

GUWAN JONES

Guwan's Wave

Guwan's wave is based on the real-life connection of diversity to quality patient care. She is the Corporate Director-Diversity Management, Workforce Planning & Human Resource Analytics for Baylor Healthcare System. Her passion is connecting diversity into daily patient decisions, which is part of Baylor Healthcare System's larger commitment to quality health care. She has worked with her leadership to identify even small changes so that patients can get needed information in the right way, at the right time. As an example, Guwan said Baylor has access to some form of translation at all of its facilities, but it's important that discharge instructions in native languages are understandable. "We found out that our Spanish discharge instructions were written at college level. Most of our patients don't speak university-level Spanish, so they were unclear," she said.

Guwan and her team set in motion many discussions and decisions that are changing the diversity of caregivers and the way information is shared. She said that appreciating diversity can also influence the decisions that physicians make, such as the most affordable prescription and the frequency of refills. She explained that even seemingly small differences and decisions can translate into a big impact for a diverse patient population.

Guwan Is Inspiring Because . . .

Guwan is inspiring in so many ways. Her foundation is her passion for quality patient care, which has given her work meaning and purpose. She is transparent and open with others, and is ready to collaborate. She gave great examples of taking her ideas to other leaders by starting with, "Here's what I'm thinking. What ideas do you have?" This open sharing of her ideas built partnerships. She said after those discussions she often ends by saying, "Let's plan to work together on this." She knows that her wave needs others to make it a reality.

I was also inspired by her ease in describing her passion and purpose, which started years ago when she lost friends too early in their life due to AIDS and other diseases. She connected her purpose regardless of her organizational role. I left our conversation knowing that Guwan makes sure that her work matters every day.

Advice for Other Wave Makers

- You really need to have a passion for it because starting a change can be lonely. It needs to fulfill you in some way. Just like when they tell you about your dissertation, it better really be something you're interested in because you'll spend a lot of time with it. It needs to be of value to you so you will know you are contributing to the world.
- The best way to get people on board is if they feel like they have a piece in it.
- Even if you are knowledgeable on a topic continue to seek out new information and ideas. Every situation is different.

"You have to own what you want, and sometimes that can be hard for women. I had a boss who taught me to speak up. And after speaking with him about my expectations on a promotion, I was more comfortable speaking up on other issues. A few months later he said that he'd noticed a total change in me. And I said, 'Well, you never invited me to have an opinion before.' His answer stuck with me. He said, 'I shouldn't have to invite you to have an opinion; I pay you to have an opinion. I want you to have an opinion.' That was a turning point in my career, which has helped with my transparency—that it's a positive to have an opinion."

KATHY KORMAN FREY

Kathy's Wave

Kathy's wave is educating and inspiring thousands of women to share their stories about career and life. As an adjunct professor and entrepreneur in residence at The George Washington University School of Business, Kathy created the Hot Mommas® Project, the world's largest crowdsourced library of women's case studies. It also includes an accompanying suite of teaching tools and educational opportunities increasing confidence up to 200 percent, called "Sis U."

Kathy is a Harvard MBA and led a very successful consulting firm when, at age twenty-nine, she was asked to be an adjunct professor at The George Washington University. As a result, she frequently spoke to groups on business topics, yet after her presentations many of the questions from women weren't about her topic. Kathy said, "The female students had questions that really were pointed toward me personally. They asked, 'What do you do when you go home at night?' 'How do you negotiate your life: your kids, work, everything?' I don't think they saw too many people like me at the time and they were thinking, 'Hmmm… How am *I* going to negotiate my career with my personal life?' They had questions."

Kathy said she knew she was on to something when her first Hot Mommas® case study won a national award at an academic conference. She laughed as she said, "You have to keep in mind my level of skepticism here. Number one, I'm an adjunct professor. Number two, it's called 'The Hot Mommas Project.®' In my real job at my consulting firm, I jokingly called my female consultants, who worked for me part time, hot mommas. My students were always so interested in them and *their* lives, so I named the case after them. I think, 'Who cares?' This is what I'm going to call it. I submit it and not only is it accepted, but there's a lot of interest. I'm thinking, what the heck is going on here?" She realized that others got what her students had been saying: "We need role models." That was her first clue that these case studies, and real-life stories, mattered. Then, it was not enough to have the stories—the Hot Mommas Project focused on action, Kathy and her team developed the educational programs and learning tools to measurably increase confidence. She said, "With that, we can take our education and go out into the world, have that negotiation, support another woman (or man). We can do anything. And we can tell our girls that too."

As M. Scheumann, a Hot Mommas Project® founding case author, said, "The Hot Mommas Project made me feel like I matter."

Kathy Is Inspiring Because...

Kathy inspired me because of her confidence in taking on the topic of careers and women with a fresh look, by using personal stories and case studies gathered through crowdsourcing. She knew that women weren't looking for the canned answers; it was the stories and sharing with one another that they valued. Also, Kathy was wise enough to realize that she had her story, but she saw the impact and power of open sharing so that anyone could contribute. She used her voice and position to do more when it would have been easier not to.

Advice for Other Wave Makers

- You have to fill a gap. Picture the landscape that exists, and if there's a gap—a need—then you can be the one to fill it.
- "There were three key things that gave us momentum. One, we listened. We asked 'What do you think?' The second is we changed because of what we learned. And third, we carefully branded it."
- Don't hide behind your computer all the time—eye contact, handshakes, get out there, meet and know the right people. That all still really matters.
- Give before you get.
- You have to have passion. If you start to lose the passion, the magic potion is gone. It's time to reevaluate what's going on.

> Be somebody that others want to listen to. Strangely, they want to listen to people who listen to them. You think it's about talking a lot, *but* it's really about listening. And understanding what is going on in someone else's head and life.

LOIS MELBOURNE

Lois's Wave

Lois and her co-founder, Ross Melbourne, started Aquire, an HR software company, literally out of their garage. In fact, they went global when their office was still their home address. In 1995 they released their first product, and both decided to quit their jobs and go all in. Lois was twenty-seven.

Lois's wave was creating a multimillion-dollar software business, doing it her way. She and her partner offered free trials to learn what users said before that was an expected strategy in the industry. Then, they listened and updated their software to make it better. Lois was an early adopter of social media and used it as a foundation to connect with others—referrals, clients, partners, influencers, advocates, and friends. She and Ross built Aquire through an organic network that trusted them and their products.

Lois and Ross also describe their company as a family-first organization that placed a high priority on telecommuting and flexible hours, which allow employees to be there for their kids' awards assemblies or a parent's surgery. They believed that if you were there for employees, they'd be there for you when the business needed the extra push. They gave employees an active voice in how they grew their careers. And many flourished as the business continued with rapid growth and expanded into new products. Because of their success, Aquire was eventually acquired by Authoria, which became PeopleFluent in 2011.

Lois explained, "I was twenty-seven years old when we started the business so I was learning everything about the industry that I could, not because I grew up in it, but because I was saturating myself with it. I wanted to make sure that any answers I gave were honest so I asked lots of questions. I was not a traditional CEO. So, I just became a voracious reader and learned everything I could get my hands on. My learning curve could have been even faster if YouTube had been around at that time."

Lois Is Inspiring Because...

I think of Lois as smart fearless. She has no fear of a new challenge, but she will absolutely be smart and learn more than anyone else in a very short amount of time. Her commitment to learning and her curious nature are inspiring. For Lois, new ideas and topics are invigorating, not something to fear.

Also, Lois sees business in human terms. She is a connector and offers a hand up, makes a generous introduction, or shares a new opportunity. Her mind-set is always "How can we work together?" as well as the classic questions of this book, "What can I do?" and "What if?"

Advice for Other Wave Makers

- Enlist people you trust.
- Take the risk that you can stomach. You have to take risks if you're going to start a wave or it's not a wave. Know your limitations up front and whether you can handle the worst-case scenario or the most likely failure and recover from it, then go do it.
- Celebrate each and every success because that gives you the energy to keep going. Be happy with the little things, as well as the big things.
- Be like a duck—calm on the surface, but paddling like hell underneath. The world around you, or the customer, needs to see your confident side. I don't feel it's unauthentic to put a calm exterior out there. You'll have to learn to paddle under the water.

> "It's a matter of being who you are. If you are authentic and true to yourself and your goal, it permeates through every part of your business. Whether it is working with customers, employees, vendors, or anyone—it affects everything."

MELISA MILLER

Melisa's Wave

Melisa, EVP and president of Alliance Data Retail Services, had the business goal of doubling in size in just five years. But, her team knew that to make it happen they had to change the culture. She and her team set in motion a very clear strategy for the organization that she described as "Five in Five." They identified five steps to realize their business goals and then engaged the entire organization in making it happen.

Melisa said, "The destination was clear. We could debate how we get there, but we had very clear goals." The first step was to build credibility for the idea. The strategy was to find the right blend of being flexible and also being specific, while returning to the five objectives again and again.

They wanted to evolve the culture to be more comfortable with mistakes. Melisa said, "We had to give people a path to take some risks, which was new for us. We wanted to not only say that mistakes are okay, but we wanted to reward some risk. So we demonstrated that we meant it. We doubled the size of the sales force, changed the compensation plan, and tripled the amount a salesperson could make."

What also changed was the diversity of the executive team in gender and tenure. Some were asked to take new roles, and this group brought new ideas. And the transition happened in a very measured and smooth way.

Melisa's wave was successful. She and her team realized their financial goals sooner than planned. Alliance Data Retail Services added one thousand jobs in twenty months and over 20 percent of employees were promoted.

Melisa Is Inspiring Because...

Melisa's blend of bold leadership with crisp and simple clarity around her goals is inspiring. Her business goal was to dramatically grow the business, but she and her team identified the cultural changes needed to make it a reality. Matching aggressive plans with bold moves within the organization had a big impact; these included moving to a culture that valued experimentation, even if there were mistakes. I was inspired by Melisa's energy and her confidence in her and her team's ability to make the changes happen.

Advice for Other Wave Makers

- Understand that not everyone may have the same appetite for change that you do.
- Learn to feel comfortable with ambiguity. In most situations, roughly right is okay.
- Move quickly. Get started.
- Assume positive intent. No finger pointing at other departments and groups.
- Be very focused and clear on what's important and what isn't. You can't do everything—know what matters.
- Build trust and credibility for your ideas very early on.

> "We had some very big goals to achieve. We identified five priorities to drive doubling our business in five years. We could debate how to get there, but the goal was very clear. It was simple, understandable, and none of us could get distracted. It eliminated any pretense."

JONATHAN MORRIS

Jonathan's Wave

Jonathan started as the new Dallas chapter president of the Young Presidents' Organization (YPO) after a year of unprecedented success for his chapter. You have to be under fifty to be a member, so many key leaders were departing on the heels of the chapter winning the Best Chapter award globally. Jonathan's wave began with a bit of fear as he wondered how he would keep the momentum going. His answer and his wave came about in a surprising way.

One of his first actions was to look for best practices by collecting what was working well across many chapters, even though the chapters had been competitive in the past. As he talked to more and more chapter leaders, he started to break down barriers. He and others in his chapter started rethinking their definition of success. Jonathan explained that, while the organization had been founded on a principle of "others first," the members' competitive nature had gradually taken priority.

Jonathan said, "We ultimately came to the conclusion that if we can get the YPO chapters working together so everyone's helping each other, it's going to be a more valuable experience to our members. They'll meet more people, hear new ideas, and have more opportunities to learn. I knew that we had to take the lead and that there would be some resistance even in our own chapter."

Jonathan started an "open chapter movement" based on sharing and developing all YPO members rather than competing with one another. He asked chapters to sign an agreement stating that they believed in open sharing. And Jonathan led the creation of practices and tools to help all of the chapters. They changed the definition of success for YPO.

Jonathan Is Inspiring Because . . .

Jonathan broke down the silos and competition so common in business by listening to leaders and chapters one by one around the world. And his commitment to building relationships and listening had benefits far beyond his original plan.

He listened, learned, adjusted, and, most importantly, updated his thinking as much as his actions, which led him to much bigger goals. I could relate to his stories of each group doing their thing and looking to win rather than naturally collaborating. I see that practice in so many organizations. Jonathan's actions—which were well beyond his official role—are an impressive model for breaking down the silos and the barriers while returning to the original values and desired culture of the group.

Advice for Other Wave Makers

- If you think something is the right thing to do, you have to figure out a way to do it. You can start off small or big, but push the ball forward and don't let others around you keep you from making progress. Any great change is always going to have nonbelievers at first. If everyone saw that this was important to do, it would have been done already, so there will always be resistance.
- Get some initial successes. Go after low-hanging fruit in the beginning to validate your plans. And even if it doesn't turn the naysayers around, it will buy you enough time to move forward and put in place what is needed. The naysayers may just come around when it works.

"In YPO you lead other leaders, and that takes a different skill set. Everyone thinks they're right. They're sure of it. You have to learn to influence a group like this with a softer 'sell.' Sometimes they'll need to feel like they came up with the solution, regardless of who really came up with it."

TRISHA MURPHY RAE

Trisha's Wave

Christmas is for Children began when Trisha Murphy Rae answered letters that children had written to Santa Claus, which had ended up in the "dead letter" box at the New York post office. Trisha was a social worker, graduate student at Rutgers, and a new mother. She wanted to take action and help, as she described it, "the unseen working poor." She wanted to do more than donate toys; she wanted to help another mother. In its first year, Christmas is for Children helped four families and it grew from there.

Growing up, Trisha had been the recipient of a food basket as well as a giver. She knew firsthand the difference a helping hand can make at a difficult time, especially during the holidays.

Trisha, her husband, Gary, and her young family moved to Texas, as she continued the work in New York and New Jersey. When she arrived in Texas, she first went to a small neighborhood church to understand the help that families in their community needed. She began to involve people and organizations to help provide these families with a plentiful food basket and gifts for children at the holiday.

Today, Trisha has a vital network of volunteers and contributors, and since her organization's inception they have helped about forty thousand children and their families enjoy the holiday. She has created a true community of givers through personal connections, appreciation, and valuing what each person can contribute to the cause. There are many charities that need help, yet in this community Christmas is for Children has a committed group of volunteers and contributors who play an essential role in helping families during the holidays.

Trisha Is Inspiring Because . . .

Trisha inspires me in many ways. She wisely recognizes that seemingly small decisions and actions matter greatly. She explained that families receiving food baskets are often embarrassed or ashamed to be in that situation, so symbolism matters. Providing name brand cereal, which is usually too expensive for them to buy, and putting food in sturdy laundry baskets makes a difference. When you show up to volunteer, you'll see Trisha coming toward you with a smile on her face and a hug saying, "We are so glad you are here! Your help is so important." She remembers the small things and makes you feel that your participation matters.

Also, it's inspiring to see how she has created a committed community of volunteers and contributors through valuing each individual contribution, always thinking "we," hosting informal thank-you lunches and breakfasts, and looking for new ways to connect that vital community to families in need. She always makes you feel that Christmas is for Children needs you and your unique contribution.

Trisha is amazing at solving what others may see as problems. One year the need for food baskets had increased so she had to stretch contribution dollars across too many priorities. Some may have spent time worrying or fretting. Not Trisha; she quickly went to "What can I do?" She set in motion a contest between two area high schools, called Battle of the Boxes, and collected almost two thousand boxes of cereal, which helped meet the increased need. Her positivity and creativity can overtake any obstacle that comes her way.

Advice for Other Wave Makers

- Find what you love and care about, and get started.
- Think of setbacks as a badge of honor. They mean you are doing something important!
- You are going to hear no. Expect it and keep going.
- Find the unique way that each person can contribute. Everyone is different. Match strengths with needs.

"People are basically good. They want to help. They want to give and do something important. Your job is to help them find their way to do it."

LORI MYERS

Lori's Wave

Lori is president of Chase's Place School, a Dallas-area private nonprofit school serving students with moderate to severe developmental disabilities, including mental retardation, PDD/autism, traumatic brain injuries, and neurological disorders. Lori became president when the founder asked parents of children at the school if they wanted to carry forward leading the school.

Lori wasn't looking for her wave, but she knew she had to take it on. She and other parents were invested and knew there was no other place that could meet their children's needs in quite the same way. Her first reaction was that she didn't have the time or the knowledge needed. But she decided she was the one to tackle the challenge and make sure the school carried on. She got busy.

Lori said, "I looked at it from a business point of view. I'm a businessperson, I have an MBA. I can build a spreadsheet. I can't paint. I have all of these creative friends, but I don't have an education background. I saw a lot of areas where I thought we could cut costs and restructure to work more efficiently. We just got started."

Lori assembled a mix of people who care about Chase's Place School and who had the right balance of knowledge and skills. She also relied on her business skills and worked to streamline and make smart use of their budget and resources.

Lori Is Inspiring Because . . .

Lori was a Wave Maker because she needed to be one. She knew that someone needed to step up and take on the leadership of Chase's Place School for children with developmental disabilities. And, even though at first she questioned *how* she would do it, she didn't let her fears get in the way. I was so inspired by Lori's very personal "why" and how she found the courage to step out and take on a new challenge because of the importance to her daughter and her education. I also was so impressed with her practical and resourceful view of the world.

Advice for Other Wave Makers

- Just do it! Even though you can't do it 110 percent, 60 percent could change the world. Still dream 110 percent, but you can still have an effect, even if it's not exactly what you want it to be. Just go!
- Know what you don't know and find the experts who do.
- You may have to cobble together a coalition of support, but be creative on how you do it. There is a way.
- Find a way to involve people who are interested but aren't directly touching or involved in your cause. Be creative and find a way to get them involved.

> "Sometimes I would beat myself up because there are so many things that I think we need to do and want to do that we can't...or I can't do yet. I have had to learn to pace myself and be realistic. You can't always do the ideal, but you still keep going. The best you can do at that moment is okay."

JOE NUSSBAUM

Joe's Wave

In 1982, Joe Nussbaum, then vice president of the Student Government Association at Texas A&M University, started The Big Event as a way for students to say thank you to the surrounding community. Nussbaum envisioned a one-day service project where residents of Bryan and College Station would be shown appreciation for their continued support of Texas A&M University students during their college careers. At first they called it The Big Event within the team, and planned to find the real name later. Soon the name The Big Event stuck, and the project has grown to include nearly a hundred schools across the nation as well as two international schools.

It began when Joe connected with Ronald Reagan's challenge to Americans to volunteer in their communities. As college students, Joe and his team started by telling everyone about their idea and ultimately built the support that engaged hundreds of students to offer hands-on support to others in the community. Joe started a successful tradition that continues to grow today.

Today Joe is president of ACP International, a manufacturing company in Arlington, Texas.

Joe Is Inspiring Because . . .

Joe inspires me because, even as a college student, he asked "What can I do?" He thought big and then had the adaptable persistence to put it all together. Joe was generous in acknowledging all that others did to create The Big Event, and I suspect that played a key role in building his coalition. Also, I am so impressed that his tenacity and vision as a college student has had such staying power—the event is even bigger today, more than thirty years later.

Advice for Other Wave Makers

- Be persistent and stay with your idea. Expect some setbacks.
- Present your change in a way that is simple and easy to understand because you don't have much time.
- Never assume that saying something once is enough. Sell your idea and repeat it over and over and over again, until you think you maybe have said it to everyone a million times.
- Look closely at your timing to be sure you start at the best time.
- Plan to have countless conversations with people and groups sharing your ideas and plans—then asking them how they can get involved.

> "I feel kind of funny even being given credit for this. It feels like I planted the seed, and it took some effort to dig the hole and put the seed in the ground. But now I feel like I'm being given credit for the whole tree. I planted the seed, but I didn't grow the whole tree. It was a team effort and continues to be."

LINDSAY PENDER

Lindsay's Wave

Lindsay is a nurse still early in her career, but that didn't stop her from starting her wave. She began her career in the neonatal intensive care unit (ICU) at a well-known medical center in Philadelphia. Her neonatal ICU handled the most serious cases, and the Philadelphia medical center had access to the latest technology, resources, and training. Lindsay then relocated and joined a much smaller hospital and neonatal ICU.

Lindsay began to see that this smaller hospital could benefit from her knowledge and experience in their neonatal practices and policies. Lindsay's question was how. She was committed to her wave because of her focus on the babies. She knew she'd have to use every option available to her. Lindsay spoke with a senior leader at the hospital about her ideas, and the executive was receptive. She created videos that showed how a new procedure worked, joined a quality improvement group in the hospital, and asked the other nurses what they thought about these practices and policies. Lindsay eventually suggested a test to see if her ideas would work. After months of conversations, her efforts resulted in changes within the neonatal ICU of her new hospital.

Lindsay shared her initial fears: "At first, I was overwhelmed because I didn't quite know where to start. I had to think about what was most important to change first. And my biggest fear is that I was new to them and no one knew me or the experience I have. I didn't want to come off as a know-it-all or that it's 'my way or no way.' I kept thinking about how to present my ideas so it didn't seem that way. I didn't know how receptive the others would be to the change, but they came around."

It took her nine months and many actions, but she realized her goal. She said, "A friend of mine told me I was being an overachiever. I said it's because I'm very passionate about this. If you feel passionate about something, you have to keep going forward."

Lindsay Is Inspiring Because...

After my conversation with Lindsay, I sat there for a few minutes. Wow. Here was a nurse with no authority, just six years out of nursing school, and she was masterful. Lindsey inspired me because she was passionate about her cause while staying respectful of those around her. She assumed good intent by all and just kept going. It would have been easy for her to complain about how her new hospital wasn't advanced or assume there was nothing she could do. Instead, she stayed positive and persistent, keeping a dose of patience, while remembering the babies in the neonatal ICU. Lindsay's passion, determination, and respect for others continue to inspire me today.

Advice for Other Wave Makers

- Know that you are doing the right thing and that your change will definitely help.
- Be confident in what you're doing. Don't be afraid of what other people will think about you.
- Find others who are passionate about the same thing. It's helpful to have others encourage you.
- Have evidence that supports your view.
- Remember that not everyone takes change well. It takes some people a little bit longer, but hopefully eventually they will be open to a change. I just wouldn't want anyone else in my situation to ever feel discouraged because of this.
- You can't take the resistance personally. You just have to ignore it and stay confident.

> "I'm trying to set a good example and show younger nurses that you can make change if you believe in something. I just want them to feel encouraged to make changes if they feel like there's something they want to change."

JULIE PORTER

Julie's Wave

Julie's wave has been her ability to encourage her clients—including my company, PeopleResults—to embrace social media. Julie started by connecting her clients' knowledge and expertise with how to share it in all media channels. She had a strategy completely counter to the conventional wisdom, which is based on business cases and return on investment. She certainly used facts, but she reminded us that marketing is more art than science and that we may have successes not fully quantifiable up front. Her differentiator was encouragement, experimentation, and confidence building within the team and for her ideas.

Julie was previously vice president at a PR agency and then became vice president of Marketing and Sustainability for a building products company. She is now the chief rocker for Front Porch Marketing, a company she founded in early 2011.

Julie and Front Porch Marketing led us into the active use of social media for our business a few years ago. She has a passion for creative and social marketing, and rightly believed that if we embraced it we would create a platform that allowed us to share our expertise, meet new clients and friends, and grow our brand. Julie's strategy of experimentation has caused us, and other clients, to remember that we love to write, have knowledge to share, and should have fun with it.

Julie is a big champion of positivity to change behavior, a philosophy that fits perfectly with her love of marketing and use of social media to grow a brand and a business.

Julie Is Inspiring Because . . .

Julie inspires me because she is a human reminder of the power of encouragement. Her strategy is: try, encourage, experiment, encourage, try a little more, encourage, and keep going. This strategy creates confidence and buy-in individually and across a team. Soon the individual or group she hoped to persuade becomes a champion for new media. She is an example of a positive incrementalist and has a passion for the power of social media.

Advice for Other Wave Makers

- Encouragement is powerful and anyone can do it.
- Don't take resistance or pushback personally—it will derail you.
- Be ready for the energy vampires. Some will try to deplete your energy and tell you that you're wrong or that you don't know what you're doing. Sometimes you have to tolerate them, but minimize your touch points with the energy vampires. They will drain you and you have to stay positive.
- Look outside your own world. Look at other industries and companies and see what they are doing, even if their situation is very different from yours. Look externally for new, interesting ideas and find the relevance in your world.
- You can accomplish so much more when it's fun. Everyone is more receptive and open when they are happy and enjoy whatever you are encouraging them to do.

> "We overlook the importance of enthusiasm and encouragement. Show excitement in your own genuine way. It's often missed and is essential for getting other people excited about your ideas. And encouragement is lost in the world today. I don't think it is emphasized enough in business. At some point I realized that if I'm going to be successful, I need to encourage others and treat people well. And invest in them as they're investing in me."

KATE ROGERS

Kate's Wave

Kate's wave is making health a value and priority affecting everything at H-E-B, one of the nation's largest independently owned food retailers in Texas and Mexico, with more than 340 stores and 76,000 employees. Kate is vice president of Communications and Engagement at H-E-B.

Kate's wave began when the H-E-B president asked her to take on this initiative, which would ultimately affect everyone, including customers and suppliers. Health is a passion of hers so the request was aligned with her own values. Her leadership knew that she knew how to start a change that lasts, given her prior success with education advocacy.

She said that health in the grocery business is complicated and creates resistance because not every product on the shelf meets the criterion of "healthful." Kate explained that health is very personal and at some point you cross the line into a true behavior change that improves someone's health. So, as an employer, there are some interesting questions to ask and decisions to make.

Kate set in motion a series of incremental changes. The company's goal was to look at health holistically, so the team involved buyers, employees, company leaders, and customers. The wave was much more than just promoting health with employees. Kate created a core team committed to health at H-E-B and increased their involvement and communication. They created an internal Biggest Loser contest to get employees involved, introduced nutritional tags for customers (after much experimentation), helped buyers introduce more "better for you" products, and educated their leadership through a program on health.

She said they have made great progress in creating a culture of health that now affects everything they do. She said it's evident because others are taking action and carrying it forward without any involvement from her or her core team—the true definition of success.

Kate Is Inspiring Because...

I was inspired by Kate's fearlessness and determination to make this happen. She thought big and her results reflect her boldness. I was so impressed with the way she translated the topic of health to so many different audiences and helped them connect into the strategy. Also, she had a wonderful balance of determination and a focus on involving others, so that it was never just her change. Kate believes that big things can and will happen, and she doesn't let obstacles or setbacks get in her way. She finds the path to keep moving.

Advice to Other Wave Makers

- Find your allies and leverage your partnerships. Know who's with you and how to work together.
- Understand your resistance and plan for it. Solve what you can one by one. But be realistic that some resistance may not be solvable.
- Communicate a lot on large-scale change. You probably think you are over-communicating, but you're not.
- Protect your people and give them permission to take a break when they need it or to be frustrated. This kind of work is hard and your team needs to have a way to recharge.
- Be strategic and specific when you ask for senior leadership support so that they know if you ask for their help it is needed and it's clear what you need from them.

"This has been the hardest thing I've ever done. But it didn't deter me."

EMMA SCHEFFLER

Emma's Wave

Emma was diagnosed with diabetes as she was entering high school. She said, "We were shocked at first while I spent about five days in the hospital. It took a few days for my family and me to accept the diagnosis and for it to sink in. I was a soccer player and wanted to play into college, and we were there wondering, what does this mean? Would I be able to play sports? Could I eat anything that tastes good again? We got a gray 'bible' with everything we needed to know about diabetes, but we still had lots of questions."

On long rides to soccer, she and her dad talked about how to make something good come out of her diagnosis. Things clicked with Emma when her dad asked her what would have made it easier for her. She worked with her parents, Leon and Lisa Scheffler, to start Insulin Angels, a charity to help families when their children are diagnosed with diabetes. The three tested ideas, got other high school students involved, and worked with hospitals and physicians, including Emma's doctor, Dr. Perrin White.

They also learned from others, including family friends in Denver who had started a charity after losing their son. They knew nothing about nonprofits, but they learned from others who had traveled the path before them.

Emma and the other Insulin Angels attend the Diabetes 101 classes at some local hospitals, and they have met with more than four hundred families and their children.

Emma Is Inspiring Because...

Emma inspired me because even as a high school student she found the path to turn a major disappointment into a positive outcome. She was intentional. The need didn't just land on her doorstep; she and her parents spent time thinking, looking, and praying for the answer to "What can I do?" She also inspires me because she not only created Insulin Angels, but she remains committed. Though she is a very busy high school athlete and active teenager, she visits hospitals every week. She walks the talk, and families with children just diagnosed with diabetes are blessed because she does.

Advice to Other Wave Makers

- Keep it simple. Don't overwork small things that aren't that important to your bigger goals. This way you can spend your energy on what matters the most.
- Don't let your lack of knowledge get in the way. There is usually someone who can help you.
- If you have a passion and want to make a change—go for it. You need passion because you have to put your heart into it. And it takes a lot of time. The passion has to be instilled within you. If not, it won't work.

> "We wanted to test it first to be sure it would work. We didn't want to go forward and then fall short of the goal.
> If we go—we are going all in."

RICH SHERIDAN

Rich's Wave

After only two years in business, Rich Sheridan, CEO of Menlo Innovations, became the *Forbes* "Hire Yourself" cover story about those choosing entrepreneurship over unemployment. Soon after, *The Wall Street Journal* featured the unique office Menlo uses for software design and development, where there are no walls, offices, doors, or cubes, just one big, open room, in the spirit of Edison's original invention factory in Menlo Park, New Jersey. Within six years, Menlo had become one of Inc. 500's fastest-growing privately held firms in the United States. This story happened at the same time that conventional wisdom in the IT industry was that all the jobs were leaving the U.S. to go offshore.

Rich explained his quest to find another way to create software. He said, "I was confident enough to believe that if I wanted to change something, I could do it. I started this journey of education, self-education, and reading all these books. I was searching. I didn't really know what I was looking for, but I was certain that I'll know it when I see it. It's like you're in a room full of toys and you're just picking one up after another. I think that happens for a lot of people—probably a lot of Wave Makers—when you're suddenly convicted within a moment, and you're 'that's it!' It just all clicked for me."

He asked the Menlo Innovations developers to work in pairs, partner with sponsors on needs, deliver real working software every two weeks, and leave their offices and cubicles behind to work in large, open, collaborative workspace. His purpose became: *Ending human suffering in the world as it relates to technology*™ so that technology is simple, responsive, and easy to use.

Rich Inspired Me Because...

Rich was inspiring because he saw programming in a new way; it was as if he hadn't worked in the industry for years. At first, he didn't even know how to make the process better, just that it could be. Rich's real journey began with his search for meaning in his life and his career. I was inspired by the way Rich decided that meaning and purpose aren't separate from career and work. He just had to find the way to connect them. Rich most inspired me for remembering what matters in life and staying true to it rather than letting industry or business norms overtake him. He knew that if he returned to the meaning behind the work, he could create the circumstances that allowed others to do the same.

Advice for Other Wave Makers

- Find the thing that makes your heart sing.
- There will be naysayers, there will be doubters. And it'll be harder than you thought.
- There's only one reason you'll keep doing it: because there's something fundamental inside your personal makeup that calls you to this wave. You can call it science and say this is how I was hardwired. You can call it faith and say this is what God made me for. Personally, I prefer faith.
- I haven't really "worked" for twelve years. The community knows me for saying, "As an entrepreneur, I've gotten my life to where I get to work half days and I get to pick the twelve hours that it is."

"There was a deep, patient persistence that existed inside of me. I'm personally willing to play for the long term. I don't need immediate gratification on any front. So I realized that the first thing that had to change was me. I had to start thinking differently. I had to see the world differently than everybody else. These authors of all of these great books gave me permission to think differently. I came to accept that different was more than okay."

ALLEN STEPHENSON

Allen's Wave

Allen Stephenson seemed destined to become a doctor, like others in his family, but he chose a very different path. And it all started with his passion for the perfect polo shirt. Allen created Southern Tide Clothing Company in 2007, and his apparel is now offered in more than seven hundred retail partners in forty-two states.

In college, Allen spent a semester abroad in Italy and looked at the window fashions on his way to class every day. When he returned to the University of South Carolina, he saw the American fashion of polos, button-down shirts, and blazers in a new way. Allen said, "In Italy I had seen how they made clothing really fit and with very high quality. I came home to this American style I'd grown up with, and it was just vivid. Yet, at the same time, the fit was off, the colors didn't quite look right together, and the look wasn't as becoming as it could be. When I saw all that, I said that's what I've gotta do."

His vision was the perfect polo shirt, one that fit flawlessly at every size, with fabric that was comfortable on the inside and the outside, and that looked great. Earlier he had taken apart shirts and reconstructed them to fit better, much like he had rebuilt an old jeep in high school to incorporate his new design ideas. He had an eye for design.

When Allen left college to start Southern Tide he had no formal business or design experience and no production or retail knowledge. Yet he jumped in with confidence. He started by meeting hundreds of people, often five or six a day, to seek advice, information, and introductions. Once he had created some samples, he shared them at no cost with key stores, such as M. Dumas & Sons in Charleston, South Carolina, to hear the reaction of employees and customers. This was the first step in building the momentum for Southern Tide's growth.

Southern Tide has expanded from polo shirts to a full clothing line for men and home items, and has been recognized on *Forbes's* annual list of America's most promising companies and the Inc. 500 list of the fastest-growing companies.

Allen Is Inspiring Because...

Allen is inspiring because he had the vision to see something familiar, a polo shirt, in a very new way. He was fearless and put so much on the line at such a young age, with absolutely no experience. Yet he built so much knowledge quickly, built a community of partners, and made his wave happen through his persistence and sheer hard work. I left our conversation thinking, if Allen, as a college student, was able to start a wave through insight and determination, we can too. My son, Patrick, was already a Southern Tide fan, and I suspect that anyone who spends time with Allen will become one too.

Advice for Other Wave Makers

- Decide right up front that it's going to happen; otherwise, it's not going to happen the way you want it to. Say, ' "I'm going to do this." It may not be exactly what you expected or decided, but you'll get there. There have been very few things ever accomplished without someone first deciding to accomplish them.
- Listen to as many people as possible. But if someone tells you, "Hey, you shouldn't do that," you shouldn't just stop. Because people will.

> "I wasn't prepared for the specifics of running the business at first, but I was prepared to handle whatever was next. I didn't really envision exactly how it would all go down. Early on, I never considered how to make invoices and ship shirts. That wasn't the point yet. The point was to get the approval for the shirts."

BOB WRIGHT

Bob's Wave

In 2010, Bob created the bigBANG! in Dallas while a leader in the Dallas Social Ventures Partnership. DSVP's mission is to enable nonprofits through donations and a venture capitalist model. Partners give at least $5,000 annually, pool the money, and then invest their money and time in selected nonprofits. The big-BANG! originated to expand the engagement and connection across the community. They call it a social innovation conference, a jam-packed symposium that is a combination of think tank and forum of ideas for philanthropists, venture capitalists, and anyone ready to learn about nonprofits and connecting business to the community.

When Bob, then the CEO of a computer-game company, cofounded DSVP, he wanted to throw out the traditional approaches to philanthropy. His spirit of innovation continued with the creation of the bigBANG! ten years later.

Bob said, "We were approaching our tenth anniversary of Dallas Social Venture Partners and we wanted to acknowledge it. But, we didn't want to just throw some big party. We wanted do something that, while celebratory, also has lasting impact." The bigBANG! was their way to engage a new generation of social innovators and encourage them to bring their talents to the community—not just for one event, but in an ongoing way.

Bob Is Inspiring Because . . .

Bob was unencumbered by the way things have always been done. He saw what could be. He is also very progressive and wanted to create a unique event that was the beginning of a relationship, not a one-time thing. And he didn't want to own it. He was wise enough to know that the only way he would realize the impact he wanted was to let go of the bigBANG! Create it and start it, but do it in a way that everyone else felt they started it too, and there would be many fingerprints on it when it emerged. It's inspiring how he kept the longer-term goals of building interest and commitment in mind rather than feeding his own ego or needing to be in charge.

Advice to Other Wave Makers

- Find a partner. Find someone who is fun to work with. Because it will be lonely at times. But that loneliness can give you some freedom too.
- Ideate and talk to a few others you trust. Consider the possibilities without asking for permission.
- Know the difference between starting something and owning it.
- If it's not fun, stop! Have a great sense of humor because almost nothing is that serious.
- Get out of that mind-set of command and control. Crowdsource ideas. Get everybody involved. Try a different angle to attract diverse populations and skills.

"This is not something we want to own. We're happy to carry the flag for this year, but we're looking for community partners to do this with us. And, it's evolved because this year the bigBang! is being jointly sponsored by DSVP and the United Way and that's consistent with what we said all along. It was for the community by the community. We started it, but we didn't want to own it. "

CYNTHIA YOUNG

Cynthia's Wave

Cynthia had spent much of her career at Southwest Airlines when she moved to an energy company, where she brought her passion for servant leadership and for translating that into improved customer experience and business results.

She headed up Service, as well as several other corporate functions, and took on the challenge of a culture change, though she didn't call it that at the time. She transformed a call center into a true customer- and employee-centric environment while more than doubling the size of the operation in less than three years. Even during this period of change, she increased employee engagement and reduced call center turnover from 35 percent to single digits. At the same time, the call center climbed the JD Powers Customer Service Rankings, and was recognized as the #1 in customer satisfaction in the New York market in 2013. Cynthia also took on many other changes, including creating an interactive intranet for faster and more accurate information sharing between departments and sites; business briefings that increased ownership thinking; enrichment of employee benefits packages while keeping costs flat; a new profit-sharing plan; an overhauled training function that supported her strategy; and recognition and reward programs that fostered employee engagement and motivation.

Cynthia Is Inspiring Because...

Cynthia embodies her belief in servant leadership, an approach that shares power, puts the needs of others first, and helps people develop and perform as well as possible. But, she is also very business minded and focused on outcomes, She believes that servant leadership translates into real results for the organization and those who work there because she has seen it. Her conviction, confidence, and passion for treating others with respect and caring are inspiring. She lives the philosophy that people make any business.

Advice for Other Wave Makers

- Know what parts of your change require leadership support and figure out how (and if) you can get it early on.
- Know within yourself why you are trying to change things and be comfortable that it's not self-serving. Know why *you* want this change. If you're comfortable that you're doing the right thing for the right reasons, do it! Just get in and do it!
- Relationships are huge! So much goes back to relationships—trust, authenticity, credibility.
- Make sure your change is aligned with the values of the group you are part of.
- Be prepared that not everything is going to turn out right—it just won't. That doesn't mean your overall strategy is off, just because one tactic was. Learn, course correct, and stay with it.

"I had been at Southwest Airlines for twenty-one years and I was well aware of the connection between business results and servant leadership. Not only are those two things not mutually exclusive, they are mutually dependent. I knew if we could get servant leadership instituted and integral to how they [the call center] operated, that customer service and customer retention would go up. I never questioned that because I had seen it and experienced it."

CONCLUSION

Be the One

I hope that *Make Waves* has given you new ideas and the confidence to go for your wave. We all have them. After a year of research, I believe that those who start successful waves believe in themselves, in their change, and in others. It takes all three to pull off a sustainable wave.

Figure C–1: Ingredients for Starting a Meaningful Wave

Explore "What if?" What if we use technology to make life simpler for our customers? What if we help the homeless in our community? What if I start my business with products that I think people will love? What if I change my career and change life for my family? Find *your* what if. And, as we always do, ask, "What can I do?"

Finally, ask, "Why not me?" If you look at the trifecta of belief in self, belief in your change, and belief in others, what is working for you that you can build upon? Where can you put your energy to give you the greatest opportunity to be successful?

Make a plan. Identify the three actions you plan to take this week to get started.

1.
2.
3.

I love the quote by Tom Ziglar, "Change starts with you, but it doesn't start until you do." Until you change, until you act, until you get started.

I am cheering you on from the sidelines. Get started. Make the difference that only you can make.

Be the one.

Notes

CHAPTER 1

1. Whitney Johnson, "Millenials and the Innovator's Dilemma," Forbes, 11/30/2013, http://www.forbes.com/sites/ruchikatulshyan/2013/09/30/millennials-and-the-innovators-dilemma/.

CHAPTER 2

1. Clayton M. Christensen, Jeff Dyer, and Hal Gregersen, *Innovator's DNA: Mastering the Five Skills of Disrupting Innovators* (Boston: Harvard Business Press, 2011).
2. *A League of Their Own*, directed by Penny Marshall, 1992, Sony/ Columbia.
3. Brené Brown, PhD, *Daring Greatly* (New York: Gotham, 2012), pp. 24-25.
4. Peter Block, *Community: The Structure of Belonging* (San Francisco: Berrett-Koehler Publishers, 2008), p. 48.
5. Stephen Covey, *The Speed of Trust* (New York: Free Press, 2006), 13.

CHAPTER 3

1. Professor Nerdster, *"Freakonomics Revisited—The unexpected correlations"*, *Professor Nerdster* blog. February 24,2013, accessed October 15, 2013. http://professornerdster.com/freakonomics -revisited/.
2. *CBS Evening News*, October 4, 2013.
3. Michael Lewis, *Moneyball: The Art of Winning an Unfair Game* (New York: W. W. Norton & Company, 2003), pp. 63-64.

CHAPTER 4

1. Roy F. Baumeister, Kathleen D. Vohs, Jennifer L. Aaker, and Emily N. Garbinski, "Some Key Differences between a Happy Life and a Meaningful Life," *Journal of Positive Psychology* (2013): 15.
2. Adam Grant, *Give and Take: A Revolutionary Approach to Success.* (New York: Viking Adult, 2013), p. 21.
3. Paul Taylor and Scott Keeter, "Millennials Confident. Connected. Open to Change." Pew Research Center, 2010. Accessed September 9, 2013.
4. "Encore Career Choices: Purpose, Passion and a Paycheck In a Tough Economy," MetLife Foundation Report based on research by Penn Schoen Berland. November 28, 2011
5. Seth Godin, "Authenticity," *Seth Godin* blog. February 16, 2009, accessed October 1, 2013, http://sethgodin.typepad.com/seths_blog/2009/02/authenticity.html.
6. Harald Weinreich, Hartmut Obendorf, Eelco Herder, and Matthias Mayer, "Not Quite the Average: An Empirical Study of Web Use," *ACM Transactions on the Web,* vol. 2, no. 1 (February 2008), article #5.
7. KISSmetrics analytics report, 2013.
8. Glenn Engler, "Snackable Content: The Key to Engagement," August 30, 2011, http://www.marketingprofs.com/articles/2011/5791/snackable-content-the-key-to-engagement.
9. Engler, "Snackable Content."

10. KISSmetrics analytics report, 2013.

11. M Booth Infographic: Source: Simply Measured, 2013.

12. Nick Ayala, "Disney's MagicBand Opens Door to Hyper- and Predictive Personalization—and Privacy Fears," January 17, 2013, http://www.jwtintelligence.com/2013/01/disneys-magicband -opens-door-hyper-predictive-personalization-and-privacy-fears/#axzz2h2txeNQF.

13. Ernst & Young, "This Time It's Personal: From Consumer to Co-Creator," March 15, 2012, http://emergingmarkets.ey.com/wp-content/uploads/downloads/2012/03/Customer-Barometer _V11.pdf.

14. Nielsen Global Online Consumer Survey, 2009.

15. CNN Money, "Kryptonite Scrambles to Find Solution," September 17, 2004.

16. Jessica Vaughn, " 'Embracing Analog': JWT's Ann Mack Presents at SXSW," March 11, 2013, http://www.jwtintelligence. com/2013/03/embracing-analog-jwts-ann-mack-presents-sxsw-2/#axzz2h2txeNQF.

17. Jessica Vaughn, " 'Embracing Analog.' "

18. John Kotter, "Is Hierarchy an Obstacle to Innovation," Forbes.com, October 1, 2012, http:// www.forbes.com/sites/johnkotter/2012/10/01/is-hierarchy-an-obstacle-to-innovation//

19. Julie Wulf, "The Flattened Firm—Not as Advertised," *California Management Review* (May 2012): 12.

20. Steven Johnson, "Peer Power, from Potholes to Patents," *The Wall Street Journal,* September 21, 2012, http://online.wsj.com/article/SB10000872396390444165804578008511493789642. html.

21. Rachel Botsman and Roo Rogers, *What's Mine Is Yours* (New York: HarperBusiness, 2010), p. xvii.

22. Aon, *Aon Consulting's 2009 Benefits and Talent Survey,* vol. 1, issue 4, (2009): 3.

23. Kenneth Rapoza, "One in Five Americans Work from Home," Forbes.com, February 18, 2013, http://www.forbes.com/sites/kenrapoza/2013/02/18/one-in-five-americans-work-from -home-numbers-seen-rising-over-60/.

24. Meister and Willyerd, *The 2020 Workplace*, p. 5.

25. Meister and Willyerd, *The 2020 Workplace*, pp. 19-20.

CHAPTER 5

1. Douglas MacMillan, *"Doodling for Profits", BloombergBusinessweek.* February 20, 2008. http://www.businessweek.com/stories/2008-02-20/doodling-, profitsbusinessweek-business -news-stock-market-and-financial-advice; Accessed September 18, 2013.

2. Alan Siegel and Irene Etzkorn, *Simple: Conquering the Crisis of Complexity* (New York: Twelve, 2013), XX.

CHAPTER 6

1. Tina Fey, *Bossypants* (New York: Little, Brown & Co., 2011), p. 123.

2. Sim Sitkin, "Learning Through Failure: The Strategy of Small Losses," *Research in Organizational Behavior Vol. 14* (1992): 231–266.

3. Jonah Berger, *Contagious: Why Things Catch On* (London: Simon & Schuster, 2013), p. 7.

CHAPTER 7

1. Guy Kawasaki, "The Art of Creating a Community," *How to Change the World* blog, February 14, 2006, http://blog.guykawasaki.com/2006/02/the_art_of_crea.html

2. Jonah Berger, *Contagious: Why Things Catch On* (New York: Simon & Schuster, 2013), p. 23.

3. Brian Fugere, Chelsea Hardaway, and Jon Warshawsky, *Why Business People Speak Like Idiots: A Bullfighter's Guide* (New York: Free Press, 2005), p. 1.

4. Fugere, Hardaway, and Warshawsky, *Why Business People Speak Like Idiots: A Bullfighter's Guide*, pp. 4-6.

CHAPTER 8

1. Tom Rath, *StrengthsFinder 2.0* (New York, Gallup Press, 2007), p. 7.

2. David Armano, "Move over Entrepreneurs, Here Come the Intrapreneurs," Forbes.com, May 21, 2102, http://www.forbes.com/sites/onmarketing/2012/05/21/move-over-entrepreneurs -here-come-the-intrapreneurs.

3. Armano, "Move over Entrepreneurs, Here Come the Intrapreneurs."

CHAPTER 9

1. Stephen Covey, *7 Habits of Highly Effective People* (New York, Simon & Schuster, 1989), pp. 81-86.

2. Covey, *7 Habits of Highly Effective People*, pp. 81-86.

3. Michelle Kerns, "30 Famous Authors Whose Works Were Rejected," *The Examiner*, March 20, 2009, http://www.examiner.com/article/30-famous-authors-whose-works-were-rejected -repeatedly-and-sometimes-rudely-by-publishers.

4. Tory Johnson, *Spark and Hustle Newsletter*, November 9, 2013.

CHAPTER 10

1. Kate O'Keeffe, "Unleashing Inclusive Innovation at Cisco," *M-Prize,* January 7, 2013, http:// www.mixprize.org/story/unleashing-inclusive-innovation.

2. O'Keeffe, "Unleasing Inclusive Innovation at Cisco."

3. Richard Stengel, interviewed by John Carlin, PBS.org, Accessed October 10, 2013http://www. pbs.org/wgbh/pages/frontline/shows/mandela/interviews/stengel.html.

References

"A League of Their Own," directed by Penny Marshall. (1992) Sony/ Columbia.

Aon, Aon Consulting's 2009 Benefits and Talent Survey, vol. 1, issue 4, (2009): 3.

Armano, David. "Move over Entrepreneurs, Here Come the Intrapreneurs," *Forbes.com*. May 21, 2102. http://www.forbes.com/sites/onmarketing/2012/05/21/move-over-entrepreneurs-herecome-the-intrapreneurs.

Ayala , Nick. "Disney's MagicBand Opens Door to Hyper-and Predictive Personalization—and Privacy Fears." January 17, 2013. http://www.jwtintelligence.com/2013/01/disneys-magicband-opens-door-hyper-predictive-personalization-and-privacy-fears/#axzz2h2txeNQF.

Baumeister, Roy F., Kathleen D. Vohs, Jennifer L. Aaker, and Emily N. Garbinski, "Some Key Differences between a Happy Life and a Meaningful Life." *Journal of Positive Psychology* (2013): 15.

Berger, Jonah. *Contagious: Why Things Catch On.* London: Simon & Schuster, 2013.

Block, Peter. *Community: The Structure of Belonging.* San Francisco: Berrett-KoehlerPublishers, 2008.

Botsman, Rachel and Roo Rogers. *What's Mine Is Yours.* New York: HarperBusiness, 2010.

Brown, Brené, PhD. *Daring Greatly.* New York: Gotham, 2012.

CBS Evening News, October 4, 2013.

Christensen, Clayton, Jeff Dyer, and Hal Gregersen, *Innovator's DNA: Mastering the Five Skills of Disrupting Innovators.* Boston: Harvard Business Press, 2011.

Covey, Stephen. *The Speed of Trust.* New York: Free Press, 2006.

Covey, Stephen. *7 Habits of Highly Effective People.* New York, Simon & Schuster, 1989.

CNN Money, "Kryptonite Scrambles to Find Solution," September 17, 2004.

Ernst & Young, "This Time It's Personal: From Consumer to Co-Creator." March 15, 2012. http://emergingmarkets.ey.com/wp-content/uploads/downloads/2012/03/Customer-Barometer_V11.pdf.

Engler, Glenn. "Snackable Content: The Key to Engagement." Accessed August 30, 2011. http://www.marketingprofs.com/articles/2011/5791/snackable- content-the-key-to-engagement.

Fey, Tina. *Bossypants.* New York: Little, Brown & Co., 2011.

Fugere, Brian, Chelsea Hardaway, and Jon Warshawsky. *Why Business People Speak Like Idiots: A Bullfighter's Guide.* New York: Free Press, 2005.

Godin, Seth. "Authenticity." Seth Godin blog. February 16, 2009, accessed October 1, 2013. http://sethgodin.typepad.com/seths_blog/2009/02/authenticity.html.

Grant, Adam. *Give and Take: A Revolutionary Approach to Success.* New York: Viking Adult, 2013.

Johnson, Steven. "Peer Power, from Potholes to Patents." *The Wall Street Journal*, September 21, 2012. http://online.wsj.com/article/SB10000872396390444165804578008511493789642.html.

Johnson, Tory. *Spark and Hustle Newsletter.* November 9, 2013. www.sparkandhustle.com.

Johnson, Whitney. "Millenials and the Innovator's Dilemma." *Forbes* (2013) http://www.forbes.com/sites/ruchikatulshyan/2013/09/30/millennials-and-the-innovators-dilemma/.

Kawasaki, Guy. "The Art of Creating a Community." *How to Change the World* blog, February 14, 2006. http://blog.guykawasaki.com/2006/02/the_art_of_crea.html 195456 i-xvi 1-240 r0rp.indd 218 1/20/14 9:08:08 PM

Kerns, Michelle. "30 Famous Authors Whose Works Were Rejected." *The Examiner*, March 20, 2009. http://www.examiner.com/article/30-famous-authors-whose-works-were-rejected-repeatedly-and-sometimes-rudely-by-publishers.

Kotter, John. "Is Hierarchy an Obstacle to Innovation." Forbes.com, October 1, 2012, http://www.forbes.com/sites/johnkotter/2012/10/01/is-hierarchy-an-obstacle-to-innovation//.

Lewis, Michael. *Moneyball: The Art of Winning an Unfair Game.* New York: W. W. Norton &Company, 2003.

M Booth Infographic: Source: Simply Measured, 2013

MacMillan, Douglas. "Doodling for Profits." *BloombergBusinessweek*. February 20, 2008. http://www.businessweek.com/stories/2008-02-20/doodling-,profitsbusinessweek-business- news-stock-market-and-financial-advice; Accessed September 18, 2013.

MetLife Foundation. "Encore Career Choices: Purpose, Passion and a Paycheck In a Tough Economy." Report based on research by Penn Schoen Berland. November 28, 2011.

Nerdster, Professor. "Freakonomics Revisited—The unexpected correlations." *Professor Nerdster* blog. Accessed October 15, 2013. http://professornerdster.com/freakonomics- revisited/.

Nielsen Global Online Consumer Survey, 2009.

O'Keeffe, Kate. "Unleashing Inclusive Innovation at Cisco." *M-Prize.* January 7, 2013. http://www.mixprize.org/story/unleashing-inclusive-innovation.

Rapoza, Kenneth. "One in Five Americans Work from Home." *Forbes.com* February 18, 2013. http://www.forbes.com/sites/kenrapoza/2013/02/18/one-in-five-americans-work-from- home-numbers-seen-rising-over-60/.

Rath, Tom. *StrengthsFinder 2.0.* New York: Gallup Press, 2007.

Siegel, Alan and Irene Etzkorn. *Simple: Conquering the Crisis of Complexity.* ew York: Twelve, 2013.

Sitkin, Sim. "Learning Through Failure: The Strategy of Small Losses." *Research in Organizational Behavior* Vol. 14 (1992): 231–266.

Stengel, Richard. Interviewed by John Carlin. PBS.org. Accessed October 10, 2013. http://www.pbs.org/wgbh/pages/frontline/shows/mandela/interviews/stengel.html.

Taylor, Paul and Scott Keeter. "Millennials Confident. Connected. Open to Change." *Pew Research Center*, 2010. Accessed September 9, 2013.

Vaughn, Jessica. "'Embracing Analog': JWT's Ann Mack Presents at SXSW." March 11, 20113, http://www.jwtintelligence.com/2013/03/embracing-analog-jwts-ann-mack-presents-sxsw-2/#axzz2h2txeNQF.

Weinreich, Harald, Hartmut Obendorf, Eelco Herder, and Matthias Mayer. "Not Quite the Average: An Empirical Study of Web Use." *ACM Transactions on the Web*, vol. 2, no. 1 (February 2008). article #5. KISSmetrics analytics report, 2013

Wulf, Julie. "The Flattened Firm—Not as Advertised." *California Management Review* (May 2012): 12.

Index

About the Author

Patti Johnson is an author, instructor, and the CEO of PeopleResults, a change and organizational development consultancy she founded in 2004. She consults, speaks, and writes about how individuals and organizations start and create the change needed to reach their goals.

Previously, Patti was a senior executive at Accenture, a global management consulting firm, where she played an essential role in creating new change service offerings, global talent programs, and providing expertise on complex changes with numerous clients over 17 years.

After deciding to become an entrepreneur, she created PeopleResults and assembled a talented team of experts and trusted colleagues. PeopleResults has grown and now provides expertise to clients, such as PepsiCo, Frito-Lay, McKesson, 7-Eleven, Microsoft, and many others.

Patti enjoys being in the classroom and is an instructor on change for Southern Methodist University in Dallas and for the Bush Institute Women's Initiative. She is also a frequent contributor and writer on change, leadership and talent issues for national media, including *Entrepreneur*, The *New York Times*, the *Wall Street Journal*, *U.S. News & World Report*, *MONEY* magazine, Fast Company, and *SUCCESS* magazine.

After growing up in Ponca City, Oklahoma, Patti's home is in the Dallas area where she lives with her husband, Jim, and sons, Patrick and Will, when in town, and their two dogs, Lucy and Pawly.